THE DIVINE INITIATIVE

THE
DIVINE INITIATIVE

BY

H. R. MACKINTOSH
D.D., D.Phil.
NEW COLLEGE, EDINBURGH

LONDON
STUDENT CHRISTIAN MOVEMENT
32 RUSSELL SQUARE, W.C.1
1921

First Published October 1921

*Printed in Great Britain
by Turnbull & Spears, Edinburgh*

Preface

THESE pages originally formed the basis of a few lectures given in London at a School for Missionaries on furlough, in April of this year. It has been thought by officials of the Student Christian Movement that the argument might prove helpful to some of those in Universities and Colleges who, amidst modern conditions, desire to come to a personal understanding with Christianity. I have therefore gratefully acceded to their wish that I should prepare the lectures for print. The title is intended to mark the fact that stress is everywhere laid on one cardinal point, which may be put thus: all that Christians are they owe to the spontaneous love of God.

H. R. MACKINTOSH

NEW COLLEGE
EDINBURGH, *September* 1921

5

Contents

Chapter I : The Need for God

I

THE intention of this short book is as it were to plot out on the map the conspicuous features of the Christian Faith. There are only four chapters in prospect, and it will probably be felt that the interpreter of Christianity in four chapters is a person whose audacity is more than on a par with his commonsense. And yet there are advantages in brevity : the trees have less chance of hiding the wood.

The arresting features of any edifice or landscape will of course group themselves differently for different observers ; and, in addition to this fact of idiosyncrasy in the writer, the reader must allow for a strong desire to relate what is said in the following pages, whether explicitly or not, to the chaotic world-conditions in which at the moment we are all living. These conditions include the greater and more active non-Christian religions. Clearly our enterprise is not all plain sailing. There cannot help being large gaps in the statement : nothing more will be attempted than a bird's eye view. Much has to be assumed or taken as present by implication. I am not so much afraid of controversial subjects ; for my hope is that throughout we may be dealing, to use the language of pedantry, with ultimates rather than proximates—with the last and highest

9

convictions of the Christian mind. And unless present tendencies of Church life are altogether misleading, where Christians differ is not so much in their final convictions about Divine realities, as in their view of the ways in which these realities are conveyed to us. Two men, for example, may be equally sure that the forgiveness of sins is mediated through Jesus Christ and specifically through His Cross, while they hold by rather divergent explanations of the atonement. It is by their certainty they live ; their theory of it might at any time change with new apprehensions of the data.

One preliminary remark at this point. The world, as I fancy most right-minded people are now convinced, has to choose henceforward between moving uphill on Jesus' pathway and by His guidance, and slipping down into ruin. Not that the world ever had any other choice, but to-day a man must shut his eyes tight not to perceive the starkly plain alternatives. To carry on by the old bad principles is fatal. Merely to proceed as if the War (and the Peace) had not happened—" business as usual " and all that— revolts men who have seen Jesus Christ. Accordingly, the Faith which we shall discuss here is not one item in an interesting list of possible policies for saving humanity ; it is the one chance humanity has left.

Just on that account, Christian Faith in God and about God is a very great thing ; superficially, indeed, it is so great as to be absurd. Nothing

but overwhelming spiritual reasons could justify
us in keeping it up. We talk almost glibly of the
loving Fatherhood of God, as if it were equally
plain with the colour of the grass ; but how,
asks Richard Jeffries, in one of his saddest and
most piercing pages, how shall I adequately express
my contempt for those who tell us, in face of
the world's incalculable pain, that all things
derive from an Almighty Love ? Complacent faith
obviously will not serve ; it is an irrelevant moral
horror, a contradiction equally insulting to conscience and heart. Faith, to be faith, must be
triumphant, and in that character it is a lifelong
strain ; we possess it only as we fight and recapture
it daily. It is peace, but, as Wordsworth said,
" peace subsisting at the heart of endless agita-
tions." Jesus Christ grows before our thought
unceasingly because we see Him steadily overcoming recurrent forces of evil which are *all but* too
much for Him, and are altogether too much for
us. St Paul felt that the principalities and powers
encompassing life in his day were beings too
dangerous to be met with anything less than the
whole armour of God. And we too have learnt
that half-Christianities are worse than useless.
It takes all of Christianity, which just means all
of Christ, to make any impression whatever on
the sins and griefs of this world, on what Browning
calls " the corruption of man's heart." Therefore
it takes big thoughts of the Christian Gospel—
big, not because we swell ourselves out with them,
like frogs in the fable, but because we humbly

consent that Christ should give them to us—to beat up successfully against the swelling tide of reasons for unbelief, as well as to inspire an attitude of clear unshaken trust which shall be at once satisfying and infectious.

The aspects of our great topic which I shall venture to single out are these. In the first place we shall survey the Need for God—those elements of incompleteness and felt want in human experience which have always predisposed men for the Gospel, and to which its appeal can be fastened. Secondly, we shall seek to contemplate God as He can be seen taking the initiative to stimulate and to meet this need, acting towards man and upon man for the accomplishment of His redemptive aim. Next, we shall inquire what effectual response men can make, and have in the past made, to the movement on God's side, and what difference this produces in their lives. And finally, we shall endeavour to show that the Christian religion, thus roughly indicated, must imply or rather consist in a Corporate Life, social because grounded firmly in history and indeed wholly meaningless apart from the mutual giving and receiving of all who are brethren in Christ. Naturally subjects so unmanageably vast can be treated of only in general terms, but perhaps the method of generalisation may leave our final results in a shape which on the whole it is easier to lay alongside of the characteristic ideas of the great non-Christian faiths.

It is perhaps unnecessary to urge that at every point of the argument we should think not so much

about Christianity as about Christ Himself.
Christianity, after all, is an abstract noun ; Christ
is a person. In numberless minds what "Christianity " summons up is the idea of a very complex
ecclesiastical and doctrinal system ; and while
both Church and doctrine are good and even
indispensable things, they nevertheless tend to
suggest that which can be dissected and criticised.
Christ, on the other hand, is our Redeemer, whom
we trust and worship. To take an analogy, the
inspiration of the Bible means in practice that we
can feed our religious life year in year out on its
contents and yet find no end to the treasure ;
and in practice the Divinity of Christ means at
least this, that throughout a lifetime we find Him
to be for us the illimitable source of the life of God.
Christianity has no meaning or force apart from
Him. Hence in our religion there is no *it* ; there
is only *He*.

II

The first thing to be said regarding the Need for
God is reassuring : this, namely, that it does
exist. It is real and definitely characteristic of
man. Animals, it would seem, have no such
need ; at a bound, therefore, we rise clear of
all materialistic or purely secular conceptions of
human nature. Man is not an animal simply ;
even at his worst and lowest he is a fallen kinsman
of God. There sleeps and trembles within him a
susceptibility for the Unseen. "We feel that
we are greater than we know " ; and what we feel

about ourselves we assume, unless we are hopeless victims of prejudice, about other people. Hence we start in good spirits : *already* there positively is that in the soul which constitutes a sensitive receiving surface for the Divine message. Not only so ; this quality, or group of qualities, in the experience of man which leads him irresistibly to lift empty hands of prayer, has in it the capacity of growth. When you stand to survey it, though it were in the most forsaken outcast, you are impelled to say : " It does not yet appear what it shall be." God alone can answer for the future of its potentialities, and He does. Thus when we have brought our needy man to God in Christ, and left him there, just beginning the new life, it is with perfect confidence that his need too, like other things, will expand and develop under the novel conditions. Christ will fully satisfy the hunger he has so far felt ; but He will in addition create deeper hungers, to satisfy them in turn, and so on for ever. No man can ever close his account with God. You are never safe with Jesus Christ ; just when you think He has given you what you needed, so concluding the matter, His presence already has made you restless and dissatisfied somewhere else, and you have to resume the quest, because now He has new satisfactions in store for you. Which reminds us of the welcome and salutary truth that a study of the Need for God is not concerned merely with other people, say the non-Christian world. They need God, but so do we. They and we alike are seekers, even though

we are quite sure we have found and long intensely
that they too should find.   The love and righteousness and beauty in God that tug at their hearts
unrecognised are tugging this very moment at ours,
for in the Divine reality there are unfathomable
and inexhaustible deeps that none of us, with
all his finding, has yet explored.   Thus we can to
the very end place ourselves by their side, sym-
pathising with their felt need.   It is only because
we have met and apprehended God in Christ that
the passion and tragedy of their yearning beckon
to us with a challenge so clear and moving.

It is another question how far in every case men
understand their own need.   After all, it is not
at first necessary that they should ;   what is
necessary is that when eventually they meet God
as Jesus reveals Him they should come to recognise Him as adequate to the void in their life
which, up to that point, may have been nameless,
flickering, inarticulate.   Quite often, one fancies,
they do not know what or Whom they need ;   they
only feel that they need what will supply, or
cure, this or that defect.   In house-hunting, we
usually are fairly clear about what we require ;
we visit this or that house, with no great hope
possibly, still with some kind of description in our
mind or our pocket, which the selected building
must satisfy.   But in the wide field of religious
experience it is seldom thus ;   so that when at
length men stand in Jesus' presence and bow their
heads before Him, more often than not, as with
the Jews' search for a particular kind of Messiah,

they make the discovery that He is inexpressibly better than the vague or mistaken anticipations they had formed. But the need is there, whether consciously interpreted or latently disturbing and as yet unexamined ; and this is the main point.

III

The first need [1] we may select is the craving after a fuller and more adequate life. Tennyson's couplet, memorably expressive of this, is familiar :

'Tis life whereof our nerves are scant,
More life, and fuller, that we want.

Capacities are present for knowledge, love, action. These capacities are real, otherwise men could not continue to exist and would indignantly reject the gift of being ; but they are unfulfilled. The will to believe, the will to power, the will to freedom and so forth—what are they but so many distinguishable aspects of the insatiable will to live ? Religion has been well defined as " a prayer for life." It is a prayer acknowledged by Jesus in describing the purpose of His own great mission : " I am come that they might have life abundantly." This deep-reaching immemorial desire may take

[1] The needs I mention are decidedly not the only ones. I fully agree with the distinguished writer who says: "Men are led to religion along many pathways—from the perplexities of the moral life, from an appreciation of the facts of history, and from the experience of reaching the limits of practical endeavour, of emotional expression, and of intellectual inquiry " (J. Arthur Thomson, *The System of Animate Nature*, vol. i., p. 41).

many a wrong turning ; it may dip its vessel in
impure streams, or in broken cisterns that can hold
no water ; but in the end of the day it remains
ineradicable and commanding, and we have no
choice but to salute it as a token of man's greatness.
And religions differ just in the method by which
they propose to deal with it.   That method may be
to extinguish the thirst for life, as in Buddhism ;
or it may be to evoke and ennoble and attach it
to infinite sources of satisfaction, as in Christianity.
Either way, the problem cannot be evaded.   For
this boundless desire is no accident of human
nature : it is constitutive.

> Our destiny, our being's heart and home
> Is with Infinite, and only there ;
> With hope it is, hope that can never die,
> Effort, and expectation, and desire,
> And something ever more about to be.

The felt immensity of the soul, cabined in a world
too small for it—this is one throbbing nerve of
religious impulse.   Our reach exceeds our grasp.
We are prisoners—all men feel this in clear hours—
of a system which we have outgrown.   Man by
intrinsic rights of being ought not to be captive
of the world, yet he is precisely that.   He is made
for glad, free personality, but often he feels himself
no better than a thing, flotsam, a link in a chain.
Quite apart from positive tangible calamities like
losing their health, or having their house burnt
down, or their money made away with, those who
take time for thought feel depressed by the circumstance that the world does not and cannot give

B

the human spirit elbow-room. They cannot breathe
with freedom ; something in life's atmosphere,
when it is merely lived according to nature, chokes
them.   Because eternity has been set in their
heart, time is not enough.   Somewhere or other
they must break through to liberty, and fill the
lungs with free, transcendent airs.

Now Christians believe that they know how this
feeling of captivity and limitation is to be ex-
plained : they put it down simply to the fact that,
in the last resort, we are made in what the Bible
calls " the image of God."   Whatever that means,
it at least means that man is not a purely
natural being.   Physical antecedents and physical
environment fail to account for him.   Man, as it
has been put, " is not merely *in* nature, but *over*
it."   The Bible put its seal on that truth at the
very outset by representing man as destined to
have dominion over the creatures.   He is called
on to assert his freedom, and to put all things under
his feet.

For us to-day the really significant point is
this, that man cannot put all things under his feet,
in other words cannot obtain and hold the mastery
of life, merely by becoming civilised. Nature
at its roughest and crudest is a man-trap, but
nature refined and robbed of grossness is hardly
less so. Civilisation turns out to be in some ways
a greater difficulty for all higher life than the most
primitive existence, because more subtly disabling
and entangling. Outwardly, of course, civilisation
is growing all the time in technical command

of natural forces and in the comfort-producing adjustments and defensive furniture of life, yet it invariably carries with it the tendency to degrade human existence by building and "running" it on mechanical and materialistic lines. More and more the simpler personal relationships of men become artificialised; the industrialism of syndicates emerges; ambitions of power, gain, and fame expand and put on wings; new and more effective ways are devised of suppressing and exploiting one's neighbour. Thus civilisation inflicts wounds it is powerless to heal. To-day the world is on the outlook for a civilisation remodelled from end to end; the actual system of the present broods over wide portions of mankind as a dreadful incubus. Also there has been stung into fiercer intensity than ever the thirst for freedom, release, ampler and gladder life. Indeed, the menacing question now asked is : Can we civilised beings so use the world as that it shall not destroy us? Is science, is invention and discovery only one more, and a more inescapable, tyrant? Succeed as we may on the natural plane of experience, in all our relationships with "things that perish in the using," how does it profit us? Is there one who does not see that progress on that level is eventually self-defeating by the nature of the case? Does not such progress stultify itself, like drinking sea-water to quench thirst? In particular, does it not, if uninspired by higher thoughts, turn our fellow-men, our brothers in blood, into mere economic figures of unreality,

numbered tools or objects rather than friends,
competitors not comrades ?

Thus the life of man, if left to the play of
natural forces, terminates in tragedy, and this not
by accident but necessity. The more effectively
his gifts and acquisitions are developed and used
for aims so narrowly confined, the more does his
inward poverty become painful and debasing.
Much the same sort of thing could be shown, did
time suffice for a full argument, with respect to
the artist's quest for beauty, or again, the thinker's
quest for truth. It is not that beauty and truth
are, either of them, inaccessible ; it is that of
both we have glimpses which we can never realise
or fully communicate or deeply and permanently
possess. And by contrast with the riches we
thus perceive far off by divination, the desolation
of our spiritual beggary is the more acutely
felt.

These considerations reveal a true point of contact for the Gospel of Jesus Christ. In God, as
we behold Him in the Son of Man, a rich and full
experience is available for the human spirit. It
is moreover an experience in which the life of
nature and of historical civilisation is not coldly
excluded as something unclean, but is absorbed
in a life greater still ; a life where, purified of its
previous fatal self-destructiveness, it is re-inter-
preted and fulfilled in the light of its own ideal.
That word which man is so unwilling to pronounce
—the word *God*—contains the one remedial secret
for this vast human need. It alone holds

forth the verifiable promise of an existence wide, free, glad, charged with the powers of endless growth.

IV

We may next take the universal human craving to escape from suffering and transience. It might be summed up as the need for shelter. Buddhism, as is well known, forms a great and not ignoble effort to deal with this desire. And yet for Buddhism, in its original and most characteristic form, the evil to be cured is strictly incurable ; you cannot destroy the sickness except by destroying the patient. Life, as such, is misery, and the one refuge from misery is ceasing to be. Here of course human nature raised a cry of protest, not without success ; and eventually " Buddhism allowed its excessive pessimism and its denial of God and of the soul to drop into the background, and found room for trust in God and for prayer ; for heaven and the hope of immortality." [1] This does not mean that Buddhism erred in recognising the problem as crucial ; it only means that its primary remedy was worse than the disease.

The problem, then, this clamant need for deliverance from grief and from decay, remains. After all our analyses of its cause or causes, it still lifts up a bitter cry, imploring the powers

[1] K. J. Saunders in *International Review of Missions*, 1917, p. 166.

of Destiny for succour. Wherever human beings sorrow and moan and die, the need is felt. If we lay our ear as it were close to the soil of history, from every age and land we hear the lingering cry for consolation in pain and nothingness and darkness ; in the storms of loss and struggle and bereavement ; in that terrible solitude of the heart of which Matthew Arnold was thinking when he wrote :

> Yes ! in the sea of life enisled,
>   With echoing straits between us thrown,
> Dotting the shoreless watery wild,
>   We mortal millions live *alone*.

Now, what in this situation men most desire is not, I think, the simple and sheer cessation of suffering, the mere arrest of transience. It would not, by the great majority, be felt as a final or conclusive condemnation of human life that it involved *some* pain, or that in its earthly form it could not last perpetually. Men would not at heart be satisfied to be told : Very well, you shall never suffer again, and you shall live on in this world for ever. If on first thoughts men might accept this, on second thoughts they would indubitably reject it. Instinct would quickly assure them that this could not be the way out. Except in a spirit of resolutely selfish individualism, which, while it lasted, would constitute an utter incapacity for religion, no serious person would unconditionally cut out all suffering from his ideal of life. For, as Goethe puts it, " no one becomes noble without

See also ~ Brit Roberty

pain." Without pain he may become clever or
successful or renowned, but not noble.

> Who never ate his bread with sorrow,
>   Who never watched through midnight hours,
> Weeping and waiting for the morrow—
>   He knows you not, ye heavenly Powers !

No : it is something else that men most long for.
We are safe to say that in their heart of hearts
they would confidently and in a real sense joyously
acquiesce both in pain and in the fleetingness of
the world, could they but be sure of two things,
and sure of them not as reasonable probabilities
but as certainties of the spirit. In the first place,
a great and adequate Companionship under which
they could find shelter and in the strength of which
they could endure. In pain, always, it is the loneliness that is worst. The sense of being placed
alone out there, in the agony, in the darkness, with
no eye to behold or hand to sustain and rescue
—it is this that bewilders, and embitters, and
paralyses. The heart cries out for a Friend, into
whose face we can look up and say, without conceal-
ment : " This too I can bear, if Thou art with me."
In every land, under every condition of social and
religious heritage, men need this ; and even when
they cannot formulate their need in this way,
cannot really tell what is wrong with them and
what would put it right, they betray this absence
of abiding comradeship as rankling at the very
centre of the wound by clinging with pathetic
tenacity to *human* friendship in their anguish,

and by an even more pathetic disappointment and indignation when it fails them. So that there is a last need left over " when other helpers fail and comforts flee " ; and it is the need for God.

That is the first of the two demands ; it concerns the inner life. But there is a second, more outward-looking ; a demand, this time, concerned directly with the world that tortures and annihilates. In their pain and transitoriness men ask for a well-grounded hope that endurance will end in the light of triumphant possession. It would not suffice even to promise a great Unseen Comrade by whose sympathy and love they could stick out the trial, if at the last engulfing death and change were to descend upon all—if the wonderful Companionship which had been imparted were itself to terminate, and be sunk in shadows of everlasting night. Nothing that can be named or thought of must separate them from it again ; it must be guaranteed permanently, for good and all. What they need at this point, accordingly, is knowledge of a Power able to secure their true life and to place every precious possession beyond the reach of Fate, not for a term of years but eternally. Always and everywhere they make the demand upon the universe that their dearest acquisitions shall not perish, that loved persons and objects shall not eventually be torn from their grasp ; but how often, where Christ is unknown, they make it hopelessly, with a gesture of cruel and sad rebellion ! And in this longing, often shown by desperate experiments of supplication, for shelter under the wings of a

Power able to make true their dreams of blessedness, they again reveal man's elemental need for
God.

V

Once more, we confront the felt need for
that which will heal and remove moral despair.
" Despair " looks a strong expression, with a touch
of sentimental emotion ; but consider the plain
facts. Wherever you find a man—and such men
are exactly those in every country from whom
Christianity wins its best adherents—who has
wakened up to the final problems of moral life and
has committed himself to the moral struggle, there
you do encounter something for which no other
name than " despair " is adequate. Temptation
is a universal fact, and yielding to temptation and
the sick remorse that follows are also universal
facts ; wherever, that is to say, people take conscience seriously. A man does not need to believe
in God to have this experience. He need only have
become acquainted with good men and women,
whose character extorts his reverence and trust,
whose respect he covets, in whose life he discerns
an element of obviously sheer moral worth, who
act in obedience to principle, and for such principle,
if there should be no other way, are prepared to
die. He cannot gain the intimacy of this sort
of people without feeling a powerful attraction to
the best things in their life and an eager wish to
share them ; nor, on the other hand, without being
stimulated and at the same time rebuked and

covered with shame by the contrast between them and himself. In short, by the light falling from their character he knows that he is bad.

Now, there is one truth we gradually learn from observation of our neighbours or from reading the best fiction—this, namely, that the Christian idea of *regeneration*, of renewed inward life and power, while it is an idea superficially incredible, is really backed up by the deepest intuitions and presentiments of all kinds of people even in the non-Christian world. Men who start the fight for character soon make two discoveries : first, that nothing will serve their case but an inner transformation, a radical change of nature, and secondly that by themselves they are unable to effect this. And in describing this utter discontent not with circumstances merely but with the very make-up of their own being, they fall with great frequency into turns of phrase extraordinarily like the Bible. Within, they find propensities to selfishness and evil habit that pervade their very flesh and blood. No hope, they feel, can exist for them as they are. Some deep taint or fault is mixed up with their constitution. Tell them to mend their ways, to correct their will ; they answer instantly that the real trouble is that while one half of their nature longs to be different, the other half doesn't. And this second half is beyond their reach, it eludes and baffles them ; they can do nothing with it. Occasionally they may even be heard saying that if they could only die and be born over again and make a fresh start, they might have a chance ;

but not otherwise. Then you recollect how precisely *that* is what the New Testament promises—a new birth.

Accordingly the man who is trying hard to be what he ought to be is pushed right up against an enigma which to all appearance is insoluble, and insoluble not by accident but intrinsically. It is a very old puzzle. " The good which I would I do not : but the evil which I would not, that I do." The two wills, the two selves in every man, tug and strain and win alternately. As things are, the deadlock is complete. We can no more obtain a new moral disposition by wishing for it than we can by a wish obtain the genius of Shakespeare. The more we see of excellence in other people only provokes our stricter self-condemnation and self-loathing. And meanwhile we are weakening ourselves further by new false choices. Sin is tightening its hold. I think it is clear that once a serious man has realised the meaning of this situation, he may do one of three things. He may abandon the fight for goodness, and lapse into apathy or self-neglect or self-indulgence. Or he may keep his ideals, and just bear his unavoidable failure with stoicism, trying not to think too much about it. Or, lastly, he may fight on vehemently, but with the deep sadness flowing from the certain knowledge that he can never win. These three things, I say, are all possible. But what is impossible is that in such a morally intolerable position he should have a free and joyous mind.

Does not this condition of things, this wholly

unmanageable problem of being good in the noble sense of the word—does it not constitute a crucial need for God ? Once a man has acknowledged to himself that, morally speaking, he is " down and out "—in the grip, not at all necessarily of vice but of utter impotence to achieve his own ideal—once the bitter conviction has forced its way in that his own badness and lovelessness are too much for him, then a door has opened at which God may enter. Moral perception by itself does not make a man religious, but it can bring him to the point at which the necessity for religion comes in sight. And religion means nothing if it does not mean escape from our own evil. There, then, is the crucial issue of personal character. It is as old as time, as wide as the world ; and, as Chalmers put it in another reference, the problem is one fit for a God.

VI

Thus there are at least three deserted places in life which God alone can fill. They are revealed, poignantly and perennially, by the thirst for fuller existence, for rescue from suffering and change and death, and for power to win character. Other exigencies will occur to every reader. There is, for instance, the need for human brotherhood fed from a never-failing spring of loving trustful fellowship ; and this we manifestly cannot furnish of ourselves. The moral paralysis of men is more than personal ; it is social, nay, it is international and racial. Whether we contemplate at home

the " class-war," as it is called in a terrible phrase,
or the devouring rivalry of peoples all across the
planet, the failure everywhere is the same. This
was seen long before the war. People even then
were growingly scared at their powerlessness to
modify or cure the iniquity and hardship of indus-
trial life ; they were puzzled by their own apathy ;
they were distracted for a remedy. How far
sadder and keener the feeling now is, we all know.
This aspect of the need for God can never be forgotten wherever those who believe in righteousness
are taking stock of the world's resources.

Already one conclusion of our study stands out
clear as sunlight. It is that the need for God
resides in, and makes its appeal from, the entire
personality of man. There is nothing depart-
mental about it. It is not that our heart requires
God, while our conscience can proceed without
Him ; nor, again, does conscience insist on His
authority, while the intellect on its part feels no
necessity for any Divine hypothesis. Thomas
Carlyle wrote of his father that " he was religious
with the consent of his whole faculties " ; and
wherever men take to heart their own destiny,
as well as the destiny of all to whom they are linked
by ties of home and fatherland and humanity, they
uniformly reveal a longing for the Unseen, and for
fellowship therewith, that goes down to the depths
of their being and cannot be eradicated without
tearing up the roots of personality. The human
need we have discussed is anything but eccentric
or one-sided. Our indivisible nature cries out for

the living God. Start from whatever point you choose in the vast continent of human experience, and sooner or later, by mountain or forest, by moor or lake or desert, you come at last to stand on some high peak from which the coast-line can be dimly seen, and

> Our Souls have sight of that immortal sea
> Which brought us hither.

A second conclusion may be stated thus. The needs we have examined cannot be satisfied by anything finite, by anything which in ordinary language we call "Nature." Nature, indeed, is far from silent or unmeaning ; the Psalmist made this plain once for all when he wrote : "The heavens declare the glory of God." But at present our point is rather different. It is that if we *begin* with Nature, she takes us but a little way. Salvation means fellowship with God our Father and through Him with men ; and once we have settled that, it is clear that the first question of personal religion : What must I do to be saved ? is a question to which Nature can make no reply. Sun, moon, and stars cannot answer it, nor can earth and sea. Our infinite hearts the Infinite One has made first and foremost for Himself ; nothing less than God, therefore, is adequate. Religion is in no sense a sickness, but the dim craving that besets a man and so often drives him up the pathway to religious faith has points of resemblance to "home-sickness." It is the nostalgia of the soul, the instinct for a true completion of our nature. God and the soul are there for each other. " You recall," says a French writer, " you recall the usages of ancient hospitality. Before parting from the stranger, the father of the home, breaking a seal of clay inscribed with certain characters, gave the guest one half and himself kept the other. Years later the two halves when brought together and joined again as it were recognised each other and enabled their possessors to know each other too ; by testifying to the old relations they formed new ones." Thus, he goes on, in the book of life, lines once begun ask for their Divine complement. Deep calls unto deep, and the profounder movement of our spirits is like the tide that follows a higher impulse and attraction.

To some extent we can now tell what must in general be the character of the Reality that will adequately evoke and satisfy these varied needs. It cannot be anything simply negative, inducing a blank destruction of all troubled cravings and desires, or quenching pain by the drug of Nirvana. Nor can it be any impersonal Entity, for that would be death to all our hopes of Fellowship, of a perfect Object of perfect devotion, and a Love that will never let us go. In such notions there is neither life nor power. What we need, what in truth all men need even when like sick children they cannot tell where they are ailing, is a personal experience of Redemption. We can only be saved from boredom and from pain and from moral incompetence by being saved into communion with God.

Chapter II: The Divine Initiative

IN the last chapter we were occupied with certain fundamental ways in which the soul of man cries out for the living God, though often with only a half-consciousness of its own deeper meaning. It is along these lines that the Need for God has come home to men. We saw that in such experiences as the craving for ampler life, for emancipation from pain and decay, for power to stop sinning and live nobly, for inspiration to lift human society above its suicidal rancours and antagonisms —in these experiences, and others like them, a hunger for *deliverance* is betrayed which only God can satisfy. Beneath all the pathetic ignorance and misguided superstition and hopeless pessimism that crowd the religious history of mankind, lies this instinctive and insatiable thirst for God. Small wonder that St Augustine's words made so deep a mark : "O Lord, Thou hast made us for Thyself, and our hearts have no rest until they rest in Thee."

These, then, are among the fierce wants and longings of humanity. They are as real, as insistently and desperately urgent, as anything in the world. You cannot open a book out of any of the great literatures without finding them in passionate expression. Christian faith not merely recognises these cravings ; it thanks God for them. It knows that in some sort they constitute a rudimentary capacity to receive the Father, to appreciate the gift He offers.

I

But now a point emerges of first-class importance, which it is well to deal with at the outset. It is this. Christian faith does nothing so easy and cheap, nothing so specious, as to turn these human cravings into an explanation of religion itself. If as Christians we know what redemption means, we could not possibly agree to say that our *wishes* for the redeemed life are, just in themselves, a proof that redemption is available. No one who understood the significance of his words would dream of asserting : I want God, I need God ; and by that very fact I know that God exists, and that He is my Saviour. It is not to be thought of that life-and-death convictions should be built on so flimsy a basis.

For we cannot but observe that precisely this is the line which has frequently been taken by writers on religion who have been animated not by faith but by indifference or scepticism. And it is obvious that it gives away the whole case for genuine Christianity. Think of the books which have proposed an argument of the following kind. The real bases of religious belief are hope and fear. Men were irrepressibly eager to secure their own safety, in face of an inscrutable or possibly hostile universe. Accordingly they set their imagination to work, and by its aid they constructed a purely

c

fictitious Divine world, peopled by deities able to help them out, powerful enough to lift their worshippers beyond the reach of famine or danger or childlessness. In consequence, the gods are just men's wishes. They represent nothing more than our own shadow on the clouds. There is no reason for believing in God's existence except that we should very much like Him to exist. In a word, religion is no better than a childish and pathetic hallucination.

The Christian mind from the beginning has been thoroughly alive to this possible line of reasoning, and it has therefore rightly been on its guard against the proposal to base conviction merely on felt need, on even the most profound and passionate desire. Here is a hungry man slowly starving. His condition is one of violent craving for food. But that does not in the least prove that food is available for him and will presently be put in his hand. There may be no food within reach ; he may have been cast on a desert island, the sole survivor of a wreck, and eventually death may be his fate. Desire, by itself, is no evidence of the reality of its object. What the man's hunger does prove beyond a doubt is that the human body is made to be fed and cannot continue in healthy existence without food. Similarly, the cravings of heart and imagination furnish no proper or convincing demonstration that God the Father is real ; but they do prove that without Him we cannot live aright.

For excellent reasons, therefore, the Christian

intelligence has never taken kindly to the idea that
religion is founded upon wishes, be the wishes never
so noble or deep-seated. In the same way, it has
never been satisfied to describe religion by saying
that it is merely man's search for God. Not, of
course, that the quest for God does not enter into
all genuine religious life. " My soul followeth
hard after Thee," cries the Psalmist. The prophet
declares " Then shall we know, if we follow on to
know the Lord." And it has recently been said
with truth and point that " we are still exploring
God on the lines of Jesus Christ—rethinking God
all the time, finding Him out." Hence there is
a real place for exploration and discovery, for the
search after God, in religion at its highest. The
man who came to the conclusion that he now knew
all about God there was to know, would have
lost from his mind the vitalising touch of Jesus.

And yet the presence of this seeking attitude
is not the deepest or most distinctive thing in
personal Christianity. It is not the outstanding
feature of the Gospel. What is distinctive of
Christianity, in this regard, is the truth that in
religion *the initiative lies with God*. If there is a
sense in which faith presupposes and perpetuates
the search after God, in a still deeper sense—and
this we most need to realise—faith is itself a response to Him. Here is how a modern writer of
insight puts the point. " The experienced know
better than to place the emphasis on their initiative
in establishing intercourse with the Divine. ' We
love, because He first loved us,' they say. The

Apostle, who speaks of his readers as those who
' have come to know God,' stops and corrects
himself, ' or rather to be known of God.' Believers discover that God was ' long beforehand
with them.' Their very search is but an answer
to His seeking, in their every movement towards
Him, they are aware of His drawing." [1] That
exactly is the special truth or principle we shall
study in this chapter. We have to see God as the
originator of religion, as at every turn in Christianity
taking the first step, that we may take the second.
By looking closely, I think, we shall find this idea
in operation right down the line of Biblical history
and all through the structure of truth as truth is
in Jesus.

II

As our first example let us take what is usually
known as the prophetic *call*. It is found in the
career of Amos, Isaiah, and Jeremiah ; it is conspicuously present in the life of the foremost of
the long succession, though we do not ordinarily
regard him as a prophet—Abraham. In these
instances, what we see is God laying hold of a man
and claiming him. Precisely how the man becomes
aware that it is God who is thus calling, it may
be difficult to explain. To quote a great Old
Testament scholar : " Perhaps no account can be
given of it but this : that when God does speak to
a man, He speaks in such a way that the man

[1] H. S. Coffin, in *Some Christian Convictions.*

knows assuredly that it is God that is speaking." [1]
Anyhow the point to be noticed is that, according
to the prophet's own mind, his new awareness of
God is *given* to him ; he does not work it up. No
prophet ever lived for whom the first event in his
prophetic experience was not his being seized by
God and turned aside from the common path and
forced to cry, " Woe is me if I preach not the
gospel." The prophet, in short, is one who has
been *called*, not by way of auto-suggestion but by
God. That at least is his own perfectly clear
conviction, and really one cannot see why he should
not know best. The words of Jeremiah are a type
for all the prophets : " If I say, I will not make
mention of Him, nor speak any more in His name,
then there is in mine heart as it were a burning fire
shut up in my bones, and I am weary with for-
bearing, and I cannot contain."

No one can miss the consciousness of higher
constraint which these words reveal. God has
come to the man and made on his mind an overwhelming impression. He has not sought the call ;
indeed, the prophets invariably shrink from the
responsibility of the Divine challenge, as Moses
did when bidden to lead the Israelites out of
Egypt ; and God is pictured as, so to speak, arguing
with them, removing their fears, pledging to them
His powerful aid. They have not chosen Him,
but He has chosen them and ordained them.
The initiative is with God ; and precisely for that

[1] A. B. Davidson.

reason, because of their inner certainty that the
call is not a self-produced illusion but an irresistible
Divine summons, they can trust themselves to it
implicitly. It is God who is responsible, not they.
We owe much of the incomparable majesty of the
Bible to this sense, which pervades the whole book,
that no one less than God Himself is behind all
genuine religion.

One manifest result of this sense of God's
priority of action is to destroy in the prophetic
mind the last trace of pride. It is true that the
prophet is marked by a high self-consciousness in
the sense that he is constantly and overpoweringly
aware of being God's messenger. The commission
is one which he dare not refuse and which, as for
example in the case of Jeremiah, insists on being
put in execution even at the price of his being
accused of treason to his country. This, however,
is a consciousness of his message, not of himself.
The prophet never is a self-made man. Had he
attained to knowledge of God's will by hard
thinking, or as reward for exceptional virtue, he
might have been tempted to vanity and have
yielded to the temptation. But no such thought
appears to have crossed his mind. How could
it ? His commission, his special work, is not
owing to anything he has been, it is exclusively
owing to God. God has masterfully interposed
in his life, has selected him as instrument, has told
him what to say. All these things are obvious
on the most cursory reading of the sixth chapter
of Isaiah, that wonderful imaginative description

of a prophet's call. "The word of the Lord that came unto Hosea" is the opening phrase of another book. "Thus saith the Lord" comes like a great hammer-stroke, at intervals, when Amos goes out to deliver the message given him. God is the middle and end of his going, but very specially He is the beginning.

Now all this is not merely some queer unintelligible movement in abnormal minds two or three thousand years ago. On the contrary, if Jesus has touched our lives, there is something in it we can all understand ; out of our own experience we can draw the interpreting secret. We are not all summoned to be pioneering prophets of the Old Testament type ; but we have been *called* to the Christian decision. In no fantastic sense but quite definitely we have been bidden to place our lives in God's hand and surrender ourselves to be the instruments of His good purpose for men. Indeed there is nothing so characteristic of discipleship as this profound sense that bigger forces by a vast deal than our will or wisdom lie behind our being Christians at all. "By the grace of God I am what I am," is a confession every believer makes involuntarily. No Christian man, reviewing his own past, would dream of saying that at such and such a date he "took up" Christianity, as quite naturally he might say that he took up golf, or chess, or big-game shooting. He cannot but acknowledge that above and beyond his own choice lay the redemptive intention of Almighty God. Certainly his own choice is implied ; he was not an automaton. But when he chose, it was choice directed to the Gospel ; and it did not rest with him in the slightest degree that there was a Gospel to choose. Its reality is not in our option. When we are born, we find the Gospel here. It is no creation of ours. It is *given*, as Nature is given to the poet, as History is given to the historian. Not only so ; just as clearly it was the anticipating love of God that brought us within range of Christian influence and truth. To whatever point we re-trace the story of our personal inclinations and decisions, behind everything else there stretches the prevenient love of God making ready for our good. That Divine preparation may even reach back beyond our individual existence. " To make a sound Christian of a Hindu," said a noted mis-sionary, " you have got to convert his grand-mother." There is humour in the saying, but also there is truth. To give people their best chance of Christian manhood, it looks as if the Father went to work generations beforehand, laying up stores of family tradition and of what one is occasionally tempted to call " hereditary grace "—stores on which the life of discipleship, when its time arrives, may draw.

Thus we may see the Divine initiative touching ourselves. It is a real thing in life, the most real of all things. If we are Christians now, it is because God first had kind thoughts about us and gave active expression to such thoughts in influences that drew us to His service. But a principle that so manifestly holds good in our personal experience cannot stop there, as if its sphere were limited thus narrowly. It must cover all the Father's dealings with the world. As Forbes Robinson puts it somewhere, " God has no private blessing for me apart from the rest of the family." It may help our thinking about the Christian religion as a whole if we now try, very briefly, to follow this universal principle into some of its chief instances.

III

In the first place, it is strikingly exemplified in everything that we call *Revelation*. That great word is one which, if used conventionally, may become as cold and hard as any in the vocabulary of science. But when understood from the inside, it glows with the saving search and compassion of a Divine Father.

One of the really important truths to which religious people have wakened up, freshly and eagerly, in the last hundred years is this, that God never reveals Himself to men by fostering in their minds the acceptance of certain theological propositions, which can be got by heart and understood by the detached onlooker ; He reveals Himself through facts of history, and above all through great personalities and their spiritual experience. How much of the Bible is biography ! And how utterly different biography is from mere logic ! And how much of the Bible would be left if you cut out everything about Abraham, Moses, David,

Jeremiah, St Paul ?—not to speak for the moment
of the Name that is above every name. There
must exist some reason for this singular fact that
the book which all agree contains the purest
religious truth—if such a thing as religious truth
be anywhere discoverable—should be so largely
composed of the records of human life, human
experience, human adventures in faith. There is
such a reason. It may be found, I suppose (at
least in great part), in the fact that truths which
we acquire by hard thinking do not necessarily
appeal to our heart or our entire personality ;
they have no power to change us and make us
like themselves. Whereas truths which we learn
through people, through their life and character,
inevitably grip at our very heart ; they change our
view of ourselves and indeed of life as a whole.
They alter our conception of the universe and of
our conduct within it. We may refuse the appeal
they make ; we may stiffen our will to pass them
by ; but the appeal is there, and once we have felt
it, we can never again be quite the same. If we
reflect on this we can see, I think, much of what
is meant by emphasis on the fact that God
revealed Himself through history. Just because
personal character is the only true mirror of a
Person, and truth embodied in life is more per-
suasive and satisfying and verifiable than any other,
the Father approached His blinded and dying
children through human personalities in whose
experience the truth about Him was being slowly
spelt out. He *sent* these men ; creative religious

genius at least as much as any other kind of genius
is the pure gift of God. The first step was taken
from His side. The Father perceived man's need,
for He had made man and understood what He
had made. And He took upon Him to deliver
man by intervening in history through prophets
and saints, and eventually by His Son.

This idea of Revelation through historical
persons is occasionally referred to, whether by those
who accept or those who utterly reject it, as though
it involved some wholly unfamiliar principle. But
that is not so. Indeed, unless the idea possessed
some human familiarity, it would be without
meaning for our minds. There must exist some
positive contact between what we are invited to
apprehend for the first time and what we already
know. Hence it is worth while to point out that
we all of us, as life proceeds and altogether apart
from the Bible, have revelations of higher truths
which reach us through the impression made by
persons. We believe, for example, in friendship.
We are sure that friendship does exist, that its
manifestations are trustworthy, and that nothing
in all the world is so precious. Why do we believe
this ? Because we have encountered people in
whose attitude to ourselves the reality of friendship was shown convincingly, so that it became
for us an undeniable fact, even when we sought
to thrust it away. Similarly a man might say of
a comrade who during the Great War had stood
by him in a tight place—To me he was a revelation
of Courage. The man's behaviour, that is, proved

to demonstration that courage is not a mere
abstract noun, empty and unsubstantial, but a
concrete arresting glorious fact. It is not possible
to doubt the reality of bravery, once we have known
brave men. Its presence and meaning has come
home to us as a revelation, conveyed through the
medium of persons. And to mount straight to our
supreme instance, it is essentially in the same
manner, though naturally on an infinite scale and
with perfect efficacy, that Jesus reveals the fact
and significance of God. It is not possible to doubt
the reality of God, once we have known One in
Whom God is recognisably present, drawing us into
fellowship with Himself. Jesus does not merely
tell us about the Father, any more than brave
men tell us about courage ; He lives the God-filled
life before us, and by the sight we are changed.
" He that hath seen Me hath seen the Father."
God's holy and mighty love is not simply something
we are to credit because Jesus affirmed it : it is
what the entire impression of Jesus means.

Now by its very nature Revelation is a
cardinal instance of the Divine initiative by which
Christianity is pervaded. In fact the idea of
Revelation is one of those marks which, from
the very outset, have distinguished Religion from
Magic. This is how a high authority differentiates
these two. " Suffice it to say that the power
which at first is conceived somewhat ambiguously
as working weal or woe in a transcendent way comes
gradually to reflect the moral quality attaching to
man's attitude to it. It is magical and bad, if

man draws near to it in a masterful and over-bearing spirit, if he uses it but to exploit it. On the other hand, it is religious and good, if the applicant for favour and grace is filled with a spirit of reverence, if, in the Iroquois phrase, he ' lays down his power ' in its presence." [1] And when we follow up this distinction, as it develops in higher religion, we may express it thus. In Magic the initiative is with man, he is trying to " wangle " this or that blessing, to manage the gods, to influence and bend them even against their will ; but in Religion, and conspicuously in Revelation, which is a characteristic idea of all higher religion, the initiative is with God. In the Old Testament, for example, what we are shown is not thoughtful minds puzzling out a problem, and forming conclusions about the Unseen and by speculative thought struggling up the ascent to elevated ideas of Godhead, as in the great days of Greek philosophy. What we rather see is the self-manifestation of God in outward events, and in wonderful religious experiences which inaugurate a new type of faith, as well as in the minds of prophetic men who are enabled to perceive some-thing of the significance and implications of God's redeeming purpose. Man does nothing to promote Revelation ; he does not deserve or earn it ; all he does is to need it. Everywhere in religion this holds good : God is the great Doer, we are receivers.

This is not intended to suggest that you cannot properly speak of Science as bringing a " revela-

[1] R. R. Marrett, *Psychology and Folk-lore*, pp. 162-3.

tion " of God, or that religious truth is the only thing about which God cares. For if (as all admit) Science brings truth, and all truth is God's, then Science too is inspired by the Divine Spirit. Wherever Revelation exists there is also Discovery, and they both obtain in scientific as in religious experience. Discovery too has a place in the life pictured by the New Testament : " we have found Him of Whom Moses and the prophets wrote, Jesus of Nazareth," said Philip to Nathanael. But the emphasis is laid differently in the two cases ; we feel instinctively that there is far more Discovery in science and far more Revelation in religion. This may be gathered from the simple fact that the discoveries of Science do not place us in personal fellowship with God, while the religious faith awakened by Revelation does. The one resembles our seeking out a great man and introducing ourselves to him, the other his searching for us, in spite of our unfriendliness, and offering us his personal intimacy. Hence, I should argue, to explain our possession of redeeming truth about God we are compelled to lay the main stress on the Divine initiative. It is truth which we have *received*.

Thus one victorious distinction of our faith is that so far from being a system of ideas or ideals fashioned by human minds, noble as these may be, it rests on and revolves round a story of definite acts done by God before men's eyes. Revelation, in its perfect form, is mediated through One Who belongs to history, to the self-same sphere of reality

in which we ourselves live—One Who trod the
earth our feet tread now, Who lay down in a human
grave, and on Easter morning shattered the power
of that same Death which slays men.   Christianity
has in its veins the life-blood of fact.   Hence the
disciple of Christ can stand up and proclaim not
simply what he feels, but what God has done.

IV

Again, consider the idea of what is usually named
the Incarnation of God in Christ.   There, if anywhere, we are brought sharply up against the fact
that in saving men God Himself takes the first step
and bears the whole cost.   The belief of those who
wrote the New Testament is that Redemption is
as much God's work as Creation, and that His
omnipotence and love are equally involved in both.
No more in the case of a redeemed Church than in
the case of a created Universe can you reach an
adequate explanation of what has happened, except
by assuming that God, to put it so, was on the
ground first.   That is why doxology is so marked
a feature of the Church's worship.   Leave the
Christian mind to itself and don't sophisticate it,
and it breaks out in praise ; it is conscious of owing
its very existence to the interposition of the Father.
" In His love and in His pity He redeemed them."

'Tis from the mercy of our God
That all our hopes begin.

Obviously enough, man's necessity is such that

nothing less than Divine interposition could have
met the case. If we are to believe in God with
triumphant certainty, He cannot be the product
of our wishes, or of our fear of things, or of a
mere exertion of our will-power. No Deity planned
out or fashioned for ourselves could suffice. True
religion is not man-made. Here is a paragraph
upon that subject from *Natural Religion*, a work
of the 'eighties of last century now too much
forgotten.

"It is said that the theophilanthropist Lare-
vellère-Lepeaux once confided to Talleyrand his
disappointment at the ill-success of his attempt
to bring into vogue a sort of improved Christianity,
a benevolent rationalism which he had invented
to meet the wants of a sceptical age. 'His propaganda made no way,' he said, 'what was he to
do?' he asked. The ex-bishop politely condoled
with him, feared it was indeed a difficult task to
found a new religion, more difficult than could be
imagined, so difficult that he hardly knew what to
advise! 'Still'—so he went on after a moment's
reflexion—'there is one plan which you might
at least try; I should recommend you *to be crucified
and to rise again the third day*.'"

Yes, indeed! this is a lightning-flash that clears
the air. It must be so. If religion is to change us,
we must be overpowered by *facts* which we cannot
help believing and the realisation of which alters
everything. Anything else is a religion which we
carry, as we might a heavy weight, instead of its
carrying us. These facts, or still more simply this

fact, is actually before us in Jesus Christ, the
personal presence of Almighty God in our world.
And wherever at this moment glad and infectious Christian faith prevails, it is because men
and women have met with this Person, and have
found that in Him God enters their experience.
You cannot adequately describe Jesus by calling
Him the hard-won result of our search for God ;
He is God Himself come forth to search for, and
find, us.

Thus whatever more the Incarnation represents,
it certainly represents this. God has taken the
initiative for man's redemption, within history and
at a sacrificial cost. But let us recollect that when
we view Christ so, we have crossed a great water-
shed in the huge continent of the world's religions.
We have decided against the immemorial tendency
of the Greek and Indian mind, and we have sided
with the Bible. Not long since a Bengali gentle-
man said to a missionary : " It is not of the least
consequence to me whether Jesus Christ was a
real person or not ; so long as I have the vision
of the moral beauty which He sets before me, I
do not care whether He lived or not." That is
the authentic Indian tradition, and the Greek
tradition resembles it. Here ideas rank far above
persons. But the infinitely more profound Biblical
and Christian intuition is that ideas, divorced from
personal lives in which they are embodied and
events through which these persons reveal what is
in them, remain frail, shadowy, impotent. The
appearance of Christ in history, the death of Christ,

D

the resurrection of Christ—these assuredly are crammed full of ideas, but what makes them effectual is that they are great *deeds* of God. Now God is acting ; He is no longer a far-away changeless Unknown behind life ; He is present, for He has visited and redeemed His people. We have sight of a vast plan of Divine love being carried forward to its consummation. Christ is not merely an illustration of general moral and religious truths, which in time we could have discovered, though with great labour, for ourselves ; He is such that without Him these truths would be robbed of all power. When we read that verse : " The Son of Man is come to give His life a ransom for many," we know, once and for ever, that Jesus did not only exemplify something ; He effected something, or rather in Him God effected everything that counts. St Paul epitomises the truth : " God was in Christ reconciling the world unto Himself." In the Cross we behold the supreme act of Divine self-bestowal, for there God is somehow bowing down in love to partake in the shame of sin. We can picture Him as uttering the prophet's great words : " I looked, and there was none to help ; and I wondered that there was none to uphold : therefore my own arm brought salvation." It is the initiative of God's love at its unsurpassable height.

As everybody knows, men have employed the most varied thought-forms to express our relation to Christ—He the Redeemer and we redeemed by Him. The Christian tradition of saved personalities has been compared to a stream with its ancient source in Jesus ; or to a chain, of which Jesus' experience forms the first link ; or to the trunk of a great tree, springing from the new seed first planted amongst humanity in Jesus' person. Other symbols too have been used, perhaps more adequate to Jesus' position as the ever-living source of redemption. But despite these variations, note the vital unity of belief. Whatever the form of thought, through them all runs the unchanging conviction that we owe salvation to One in whom God was uniquely present in history and whose appearance in the fields of time we have no option but to trace to the self-abnegating love of the Eternal. It is just as the Psalmist said : " Salvation belongeth unto the Lord." It is God's doing, and it is wonderful in our eyes. The love of the Father is the fount of all redemption. Everything began with acts of God by which He put the whole world for ever in His debt. Now it makes an enormous difference to our view of religion whether our eyes have or have not opened to this fact. As the present writer ventured to put it elsewhere : " According to Biblical faith, from the prophets onward, the chief thing in religion is what God does, viz., seek unweariedly to redeem His children through historical experiences. According to Greek and Indian mysticism, on the other hand, the chief thing in religion is what man does, viz., avert his eyes from historical fact, and plunge a blinded and suppressed self in the moving, changeless impersonal Divine." And to-day for serious people interested in religion the alternative really lies between something like a resuscitated Greek or Indian mysticism and an affirmation of God's self-bestowal in the events of the past, on the lines of Biblical faith. The one deprives history of ultimate meaning; the other shows history as the very sphere and medium of God's redemptive approach to His children, and derives permanently from history the very life and enthusiasm of religion.

This, one sees, is of literally crucial importance for the Christian who is presenting his faith to non-Christians. If salvation is traceable to Divine initiative, breaking into time and becoming concrete in actual events, then plainly the missionary is in a position to offer to non-Christians what, so far, they have not got. If Christianity is only a matter of general spiritual truths, or universal moral ideals, it by no means follows necessarily that the missionary is able to propose to non-Christians anything absolutely or specifically new. Indeed, as Mr Bevan has pointed out,[1] it is quite possible he may find that the people to whom he goes have developed, whether owing to temperament or history, a more vivid sense of some spiritual ideas, such as Divine immanence, than he has. Certain aspects of God's being might be apprehended and described with a genius and power which is able to enlarge and freshen even the Christian's thought of God. On the other hand, just in so far as the missionary has to tell

[1] See the *International Review of Missions* for July 1919.

of certain Divine events, or to present a certain Divine personality who once lived and taught, died and conquered death, all that he says *is* new. Here he gives only, and does not receive. It is no longer a question of degree ; you either know or do not know of Jesus Christ. The fact of Christ could never be excogitated by any amount of reflection ; men have to come in experienced contact with the record of His career. Thus what we have in Christianity is not so much the superiority of one idea to another as the incomparable fact of God's creative and inaugural action in the story of our race. We are in the presence of things done by Him freely, originatively, out of infinite resource.

V

Once more, the Divine initiative is conspicuously shown in the rise of personal religion.

Every man possessed by victorious Christian faith, if in any degree he understands what has happened to him, is ready to confess without reserve that religion touched and won him by God's taking the first step, and invading his life. It makes not the slightest difference that he may have had a long search before he found ; the search is itself proof that God had first come near and stirred him, wakening the desire to seek. One recalls the words which, in one of his *Meditations*, Pascal puts in the lips of the Crucified : " Thou wouldst not have sought Me, hadst thou not already found Me."

Gaston Frommel, a Swiss theologian whose death in 1908 was an appreciable loss to the higher life of his country, gives this account of his experience :

" I was following out my life, pursuing my own desires, when Christ advanced to meet me, placed Himself before me, and barred my way. He stopped me ; He made a silence in my heart ; and then He held with me a solemn interview in which He spoke as He alone can speak. For long I disputed the case in a revolt of mingled anguish and bitterness ; for I could not consent to renounce everything which till then had seemed to me precious and desirable ; and yet I felt it to be a question of life and death, and that to disobey would have been to pronounce sentence on myself. When at last I gave up the struggle and accepted God's will for my life, I was no longer free. I was a bondman, the bondman of Jesus Christ." [1]

It is not my object in quoting this remarkable passage to suggest that every Christian's life must exhibit a crisis resembling that of Frommel. The lesson to be drawn from his words is of a different kind. They illustrate memorably the truth of which each believer's history is an example, namely, that we irresistibly ascribe the fact that we are Christians at all to the anticipative action, the prevenient goodness, of the Father. It has been *given* to us to believe in God. What holds true,

[1] Cf. *Études Morales et religieuses*, pp. 21-28.

as we have seen, on the widespreading field of
God's self-manifestation in history and supremely
in His self-incarnation in Jesus Christ, is not less
true throughout the more limited sphere of the
individual life. All Christians who cherish a deep
sense of indebtedness to God are intensely conscious
that they have not saved themselves, but that God
has saved them. " It pleased God to reveal His
Son in me," writes St Paul ; " Out of His fulness
have all we received," writes St John ; and
testimonies could be multiplied a hundredfold.
Of course this consciousness that God's love has
been the great causal agency in redemption may,
when it comes to what is called doctrine, take
very different forms. One Church will speak of
justification by faith, as Luther did ; another will
put everything down to the account of sovereign
electing grace, as did Calvin ; the Roman Catholic
Church puts forward its teaching about the sacra-
ments. But all these doctrines convey at bottom
the same thing. " They mean," as Denney has
said, " that in the work of man's salvation an
unconditioned initiative belongs to God, and that
all that is required of man is the unreserved
abandonment of himself to what God has done."

That principle concerns us all personally.
Whatever be the way God took to make us His
children, whatever our private story regarding
the inception of personal Christianity in our own
life, we feel that " He loved us first." A strong
hand was laid upon us and turned our steps to
faith. We are under debt to God—a debt we

can never repay though it is joy to try to pay something—because at the outset of true life for us His love forestalled our seeking, His hand stirred us into movement, His voice sounded in our ear : " Awake thou that sleepest, and arise from the dead, and Christ shall give thee light."

It all means that Christian faith is inexorably opposed to the notion of self-redemption. Never has it been able to bear even the idea of such a thing. At various epochs it has been confronted with the proposal to save ourselves, whether made from without Christendom or from within. In Buddhism, for example, the soul redeems itself by meditation, by enlightened thought, by sheer insight into the sombre truth " vanity of vanities, all is vanity." And of this the last outcome, naturally, is pure pessimism, such a pessimism as can only be dispelled by the exhilarating voice of Jesus : " I am come that they might have life, and have it to the full." But even within the Church the same proposal has been made. There is an old heresy of the early centuries, bearing the name of Pelagius. Roughly, but not unfairly, his teaching may be summed up in the watchword : Every man his own saviour. It is good to know of Christ, but He is by no means indispensable. It was a challenge to the very heart of the Gospel, and from Pelagius' day to ours the Church has disowned that theory and fought it to the death. How could it do otherwise, so long as its faith remained identical with the faith inspiring

the following triumphant sentences? They occur
in a Christian letter of the first century, and in
every line we hear the great note of praise for the
things God has done and will yet do.

" Blessed be the God and Father of our Lord
Jesus Christ! By His great mercy we have been
born anew to a life of hope through the resurrection of Jesus Christ from the dead, born
to an unscathed, inviolate, unfading inheritance ;
it is kept in heaven for you, and the power of
God protects you by faith till you do inherit
the salvation which is all ready to be revealed at
the last hour." [1]

[1] First Epistle of Peter i. 3-5 (Moffatt's translation).

Chapter III. The Response of Man

IN preceding chapters we have surveyed, on the one hand, the human need for God betrayed in deep persistent cravings, and on the other the Father's action as He comes forth, spontaneously and creatively, to establish new relations between Himself and men. After this study of man's call and the Divine redemptive movement, let us now turn to Redemption as an experience, or the human response to God's unveiling of Himself in Jesus. The topic is so immense that in a single chapter we can examine it solely from one point of view. A passage from Bishop Westcott's *Life* may perhaps indicate what this point of view should be. He was on a visit to his old schoolmaster, Dr Prince Lee ; and as they talked together, the other turned and said : " People quote various words of the Lord as containing the sum of the Gospel—the Lord's Prayer, the Sermon on the Mount, and the like. To me the essence of the Gospel is in simpler and shorter terms : Fear not, *only believe.*" " Only believe "—this means that the proper and sufficient response of man to God is Faith. God and faith belong together. The attempt to understand either separately is vain. One of the ringing sentences of the New Testament declares that " without faith it is impossible to please God," but just as certainly without faith it is impossible to know Him. On the other hand, faith is so tremendous a thing, so defiant of appearances, so supernatural and surprising, that you could not account for its presence in any heart without bringing in the power of God. In one sense, and that a decisive sense, faith covers everything in our experience of Christianity. It is not a particular religious virtue, like hope or kindness ; it is the basis and staple of all religion.

Prince Lee's conception of the Gospel has one very attractive feature, strongly reminiscent of the New Testament—its simplicity. For people constantly tempted to imagine that personal Christianity is quite a number of things there is genuine relief in the thought that, on the contrary, it means just one big thing. It is definable, for all practical purposes, as " unwavering trust in the heart of God Who has given Himself to us in Christ as our Father." An instinct tells us that Christianity as an interior life and conviction *must* be simple. It is of necessity simple, because it is for everybody, and Jesus said the condition of having it is a childlike heart. When we go to non-Christian people with the Gospel, we do not offer them an elaborate or highly developed theology. In its proper place, theology is right and even unavoidable, but it may create difficulties as well as relieve them. Many of us can recollect a striking appeal to the Church made, in 1910 I think, by a distinguished missionary to Egypt, Mr W. H. Gairdner, to the effect that the doctrine of the Trinity ought to be re-studied in view of the immense difficulty it occasions to the Mohammedan mind. That illustrates what is meant, and confirms our instinct for simplicity. The Gospel which saves men, and by which we know in our clearest hours we live, is not intricate or inapprehensibly obscure.

Neither, of course, is it simple in any cheap or shallow sense. It is rather as profound as life. We can say of the plainest statement of the Gospel, the least complex description of the Kingdom of God and how we may be members of it, exactly what Tennyson said of the flower plucked from the crannied wall—that if we could understand it, round and round and from end to end, we should know what God and man is. In like manner faith, as an attitude of the soul, is simple indeed, yet many-sided. It includes trust, awe, dependence, reverence, humility, penitence, blessedness, joy ; it is a comprehensive name for everything included in our experience of God the Saviour and His boundless love.

I

It may help our analysis of faith, as man's unreserved abandonment of himself to what God has done, if first of all we settle what faith is not. To begin with, it is not just the acceptance of Biblical narratives as true. Merely to assent to the infallible correctness of all statements made in the Bible does not save us ; it does not, as a matter of fact, bring us of necessity and by its own intrinsic meaning into personal fellowship

with God, which is the only idea of being saved
that can be admitted within Christianity. If
to-day we were to insist on any such identification
of faith with a confession of the unerring accuracy
of Biblical writers, we should debar millions of
our contemporaries from the discipleship of Jesus.
Biblical criticism, which is one of God's instruments to prevent people from basing their religious
life on anything but Himself, will always persist ;
and once these critical questions, from which
thoughtful men cannot escape, have been agitated,
no settlement of them is possible otherwise than
by fighting our way through to the truth. It has
been well said that what is really *fundamental* in
our religious faith is " not the many things we
try to believe, but the few things we cannot
persuade ourselves to disbelieve." Such are the
revealed holiness of God, His love in the Cross,
the unity of Christ with God. Shairp's lines come
to memory at this point :

> I have a life in Christ to live ;
>   But, ere I live it, must I wait
> Till science can clear answer give
>   Of this or that book's date ?

Then he replies to his own question by saying
that he will rather resort to Christ Himself, and
take refuge under His personal power. That is
something we can be certain about, whereas
while time lasts the date or authorship of
particular books of the New Testament may well
be wrapped in obscurity.

Thus, at the very outset, we come down right upon this, that faith in the saving sense of the word is a personal and independent spiritual conviction. It is our grasp of that on which we could stake our life; we cannot shake it off, except by ceasing to be ourselves. For the Christian—at all events the kind of Christian who in the past has got things done—would unhesitatingly affirm that his consciousness of God, his sense of being, as he prays, in communion with the unseen Father, was as authentic and irrefragable as his sense of right and wrong. At times his grasp of either may tremble, but it does not slacken. God is as real as conscience. Anyone can see how wide a gulf yawns between this sort of inward heartfelt conviction on the one side, and on the other religious ideas merely caught up by hearsay or imitated from a neighbour. If a scholar tells me that the Epistle to the Hebrews was written by Apollos, I may be grateful for an interesting suggestion and think it quite fairly probable, but I don't lay it down at the foundation of my religious life or feel that everything in my relations to God turns upon it. But that precisely is what I do feel about Jesus Christ. With Him I can be in direct moral relations; He comes in upon me imperiously and confronts me in majesty and goodness: hence what He compels me to feel regarding His power I cannot afterwards truthfully deny or question.

While, however, faith means independent personal conviction, the conviction is not self-produced. It is not, to speak technically, a postulate. If a man says : I believe this or that idea is true, because if it were not the world would be intolerably bad, then he is making a postulate. He is asserting something or other because the idea of it has occurred to him and is so infinitely and nobly attractive that to renounce its truth would be like despairing of the universe. Faith does not rest on postulates in that sense. Otherwise our certainty of God would depend really on our wishes, but as the proverb runs, " if wishes were horses, beggars would ride." So far from being thus self-produced, full Christian faith, as we have seen, is produced by Revelation. Such revelation may take different forms. It may come through Nature, as it did to Wordsworth.

> " I have felt
> A presence that disturbs me with the joy
> Of elevated thoughts ; a sense sublime
> Of something far more deeply interfused,
> Whose dwelling is the light of setting suns,
> And the round ocean and the living air,
> And the blue sky, and in the mind of man :
> A motion and a spirit, that impels
> All thinking things, all objects of all thought,
> And rolls through all things."

It may come through events of personal life, or through moments of intense rapt spiritual feeling, such as Wordsworth also has described.

> " In such access of mind, in such high hour
> Of visitation from the living God,
> Thought was not ; in enjoyment it expired.

Rapt into still communion that transcends
The imperfect offices of prayer and praise,
His mind was a thanksgiving to the Power
That made him ; it was blessedness and love."

But above all, and this is in a class by itself, it may come through the personality of Jesus Christ. And here St John has put the truth into words once for all :

" The Word became flesh, and dwelt among us —and we beheld His glory, glory as of the only begotten from the Father—full of grace and truth. . . . No man hath seen God at any time ; the only begotten Son, which is in the bosom of the Father, He hath declared Him."

But if it is supremely Jesus Christ who evokes and sustains and educates faith, everything for Christianity depends on our knowing Him, as everything in the way of communicating this religion to others depends on our enabling them to see Him. It is for us to let them see Him through our lives. But there our perpetual failure is so serious that we may well be thankful there is a far more effective medium through which they can be brought in contact with Him— the picture of His character and work in the New Testament. It is as men gaze at Him, listen to Him, bow in submission before Him, that their mind opens to faith in the Father. A world with Jesus in it, they rightly feel, is a world with a loving God over it. That is why to-day the watchword is heard on every side : a Christlike God. God, Christianity declares, is thoroughly

like Jesus ; or, to use the great words cited by
St John, " I and the Father are one." To live in
Jesus' company and under His control invariably
means a new belief in God, which steadily grows
more rich in significance and more fruitful in
impulse to serve men. No one who had ever seen
Christ in this light would dream of holding that
faith is our own creation. It is God's doing :
He draws out our new trust by coming close to
us in Jesus.

And here, it may be pointed out, is to be found
the solution of a difficulty which has caused much
perplexity. Some one may say : You first tell
us that faith is independent personal conviction,
which must be a man's own venture and cannot
be borrowed from his neighbour, and then you
add that it is God's doing. Are both things true ?
How can faith be our own act and yet a gift of
God ? But surely quite analogous things are
happening constantly. No one, I imagine, feels
the slightest difficulty in saying that the presence
of a great soldier on the field *gives confidence* to
his troops, or again, that the captain's demeanour
in a shipwreck gives confidence to the passengers.
But because confidence has been given to them,
it is none the less their own. So, too, it is with
us. God gives us confidence, that is He gives us
faith, by presenting Himself to us in Jesus. We
look to Jesus, and trust springs in our heart.
Thus, as in other instances, Christian faith is
equally both things—a gift or bestowal of the
Father and an independent venture of our own.

E

Probably the reader has by this time begun to
feel that our analysis of faith is yielding rather
paradoxical conclusions. Well, it ought to ; real
faith does have a large element of paradox. When
St Paul wrote that " all things work together for
good to them that love God," his statement was
unquestionably paradoxical, for nothing viewed
superficially could be more improbable. When we
reflect upon the appalling disasters of the War,
when we come away from visiting in an asylum
one who for many years had spent himself in the
disinterested service of humanity, it is difficult
enough to go on believing that all things work
together for good. No doubt St Paul is right
after all, but he is not obviously or undisguisedly
right. The thing is not as plain as a pikestaff.
Here, then, is the paradox that faith is simultaneously our own doing and God's gift ; the com-
panion paradox is that faith simultaneously puts
us under authority and makes us free. Both
things are true together, and the togetherness is no
accident but essential. When I see Jesus Christ—
living, dying and risen—as the revelation of God,
then I know that I have found my Master. I
cannot set my faith upon Him without being
thereby aware that I must obey Him unconditionally. Any failure to do His will so far dims
my insight into His Saviourship. A new moral
life begins for me in the consciousness, humbled
yet gladdened, of being in the presence of One
who is literally my " Lord." That is, I am now
under authority, while at the same time my faith

has set me free. To submit to Jesus Christ is
indeed the first act of complete moral liberty a
man ever achieves, and by such submission his
personality is not invaded or crushed ; it is released
and elevated. Jesus Christ, in the power of His
quickening and subduing life, is the Owner of the
soul who frees the soul He owns. In Him we find
the Authority we require in order to be utterly
emancipated—in which fact lies the solution of a
thousand inner problems and tumults and rebellions.
And this is another of the profound paradoxes included in what Christians mean by " faith."

In the religion of India there occurs a striking
conception which has often impressed students
alike by its resemblance to the Christian thought
of faith and by its difference. It is the Hindu
conception of *Bhakti*, which goes back to pre-
Christian times but has a special prominence in
modern forms of piety. *Bhakti*, which has been
defined by a Christian missionary as " a heartfelt
trust and love towards the Supreme Being," does
not mean mere belief, though belief is implied
in it. It is devotional faith in the Adorable
One, and is essentially monotheistic in temper.
Students of Hinduism lay emphasis on the sincerity
and inwardness that characterise the religious
attitude thus indicated. To be saved by *Bhakti*
is to be saved not by knowledge or by meritorious
works, but by loving trust in the Supreme ; and
it is held that in connexion with it we find a genuine
belief in the Fatherhood of God and the immortality of the soul.

The difficulty begins, however, when we inquire through what facts or manifestations the Supreme One or Vishnu, in Hinduism, is known. Vishnu appears to men in a series of incarnations, the most notable of these being Krishna. Do we have here a real counterpart to Jesus Christ, the revealed object of faith for us ? That is a hard question, for the religious mind of India has never quite settled the point whether historical fact is or is not important. Speculatively, history ranks as pure illusion, yet it is often claimed that Krishna in Hinduism corresponds to Jesus in Christianity. It is true that Krishna is originally a historical person who proclaimed a morality suited to the warrior castes, but the stories told about him in the sacred books are so unedifying that later they have had to be idealised out of all recognition. Clearly therefore the deeply spiritual elements of *Bhakti*, as just described, can scarcely be evoked or nourished by what is actually known of Krishna from historical sources. And there lies the fatal weakness. For what is to feed the burning flame of trust ? How can Krishna's recorded moral imperfections be a worthy mirror of the Supreme ? Whereas faith evoked by the historical Christ lives under wholly different conditions, for when our trust falters, as it does so often, we can restore its vigour by renewed contemplation of Jesus, the Divine object given in history for believing sight.

II

We have seen that faith is not equivalent simply to the acceptance of Biblical narratives as true ; it is equally important to observe that neither does it consist in assent to doctrines, or statements of theology. To put it concretely, the faith which redeems a man and which he can recommend to others with the certitude that they can live and die by it in fellowship with God, is not just belief in a creed. Occasionally it may seem difficult to agree to this, as people say, in the abstract, but in practice there is no difficulty whatever. If, whether at home or abroad, we were sought out by somebody who wished to learn the way into the Kingdom of God and communion with the Father, not one in a hundred would dream of giving the advice : Put your trust in the Thirty-nine Articles or the Westminster Confession. Instinctively we should shrink from saying anything of the kind. And why ? To a great extent our reason probably would be that the propositions which compose a creed are not, just as they stand, and for an inquirer who is seeking the way to God, either self-explaining or self-accrediting. Take, for example, the doctrine of the Trinity, in which we rightly epitomise the whole Christian faith, and which, if properly interpreted, is nothing more or less than a short summary of what, as Christians, we know about God. Christian men cannot express all they mean by God except by saying "Father, Son and Holy Spirit." As it

has been put : " God as Holy Love we name the
Father ; this same eternal God, as making the
sacrifice of love and appearing in one finite spirit
for our redemption, we name the Son ; God filling
as new life the hearts to which His Son has become
a revelation, we name the Spirit. In this confession we resume the best it has been given us to
know of the eternal God our Saviour." Granted
the truth of this, and that it is all implicitly present
in the most elementary Christian experience ;
still, we must feel how much reflection and conscious intentional analysis has become mixed up
with it. The beginner would very naturally be
puzzled if, at his stage, we pressed the doctrine
of the Trinity upon him, much more if we insisted
on his assent to the doctrine as a preliminary
condition of his being a Christian. The New
Testament, as usual, is wiser when to the seeker's
question it returns the answer : " Believe on the
Lord Jesus Christ, and thou shalt be saved."
That is, it goes on the clear and sufficient principle
that what alone can awaken and satisfy the faith
of sinful men is a Person. Instead of the creed,
it speaks of Jesus Christ.

Thus after needful discussion of the question
what faith is not, we come right up against the
problem of faith itself. What *is* the faith that
means salvation for human life—our own life and
society's, in so far as our influence upon society
extends. I suggest that it is *the obedient and
grateful apprehension of God in Christ.* Look at
God in Christ, the Personality whose career we

follow in the Gospels, through the Galilean ministry, on to Gethsemane, Calvary, the open grave—let that Man stand before your secret thought and occupy steadily the focus of your attention; consider Him with gravity and listen to what He has to say, and you will feel, at the least, that He is well worth believing in. Life would not be thrown away if spent in His obedience. He is great enough to assuage the need for God. You are being appealed to for faith in One who, simply by being what He is, is capable of eliciting and holding a spontaneous and reasonable trust. The object of faith is here the sufficient cause of faith, or, to put it otherwise, the adequate reasons why I should commit my life to Christ are all contained in the fact of Christ Himself. Once I have *seen* Him, I know that what I have been searching for is at last found. When my trust in Him is invited, I am not tempted to intellectual insincerity as might be the case if I were asked point-blank to accept a creed; on the contrary all my faculties—conscience, reason, and heart in their indivisible unity—combine to assure me that He is worthy to be trusted. His very meaning has power to evoke a new spiritual life. In responding to Him we know without dispute that we are responding to One who is God's representative and presence in our lives.

A moment ago it was suggested that faith is, in essence, the obedient and grateful apprehension of God in Christ. If this description is at all like the truth, then, quite irrespective of any pedantic analysis, faith obviously constitutes an experience

in which each of the three ultimate modes of
being conscious—knowing, feeling and willing—is
involved. Knowing is present, for it is an *apprehension* of God. " I know whom I have believed."
When we lay hold upon God, we are in living
touch with the last reality in the universe. The
facts upon which faith rests, and on which it is
rightly founded, have somehow come within our
range of vision. Truth is embedded in faith as
definitely as bones are embedded in a man's
hand ; mere sentiment, divorced from belief, has
always proved limp and ineffectual. Feeling, too,
is present ; for it is a *grateful* apprehension of
God. We recognise Him as the supremely precious
Being Who is desirable for His own sake and can
satisfy our deepest and sorest needs, a recognition
which sets athrobbing within us the chords of
emotion. Without emotion, which is of course
as different as can be from sentimentality, knowledge of God, if indeed it were possible at all,
would be hard and barren. Finally, will is present ;
for faith is an *obedient* apprehension. When we
trust God in Christ, thereby trusting ourselves to
Him, it is an act of volition—an act that bids
away the hostile and selfish past and opens up a
new era of ampler life. You cannot have the
transfiguring faith in God except as you long for
Him and take His promise with humility, closing
the door thus upon self-centredness and setting
wide another door which ushers you into a life
where not self but God and others occupy the
focus of interest.

Surely it is a peculiar merit in faith that it evidently gives expression to all the elements in our complex personality. Try the experiment of limiting faith narrowly to one of the three, knowledge, feeling or action, and it will be reassuring to discover that it emphatically is not eccentric or one-sided in that way ; rather it is the thankful and contrite answer of the whole man to what the Bible calls " the God of our salvation." There is corroboration of the veracity of faith in this all-roundness. As Henry Sloane Coffin has said : " One part of us may be deceived, but that which contents the entire man is not likely to be unreal. Arthur Hallam declared that he liked Christianity because ' it fits into all the folds of one's nature.' " Our distracted being has at length found in Christ that which unifies it and forms a rallying-point for every true motive and aspiration. Always where you have a man who has committed himself to God in Christ and is conscious of having been thereby redeemed from desperately real sins— changed from selfishness to love, from slavery to freedom, from the fear of things to a trust in God which cannot be shaken by any words of man or outward event—you have one who in vital principle has been brought into harmony not merely, though supremely, with God, but also with himself and his neighbour, as well as with all exterior circumstances which the Father may appoint.

III

Having more or less cleared up the real
character of faith, let us now ask what effects it
is calculated to produce. Plainly its effect will
depend on what we receive through it—*receive*, I
say, for as we have seen in religion we are primarily
receivers, God is the Doer. Of course, when we
try to define with exactitude what it is that, when
taken in faith, makes new persons of us, a number
of possible descriptions leap to our minds. What
we take, broadly stated, is just "salvation,"
personal and social ; and salvation, like a great
mountain, may be sketched from various points
of view. But there is no harm in our trying for
a quite brief account of it to which everybody, so
far, would agree. Let us say, then, that what we
accept in faith is " the love of God commended to
the world when Christ died for sinners." To see
God through the medium of what His Son antici-
pated in Gethsemane and underwent on Calvary,
and to see Him so with trust and penitence, is
to know definitely that *our sins are forgiven*. It
is to lose the sense of exclusion from the Father ;
to be utterly certain that He is such a God that
He receives sinners and never casts them out. It
has been observed that in the cross " the Father
says by His whole bearing towards us, My son,
let us share the sorrow and live down the shame
together " ; [1] and whoever has heard that voice
speaking from Christ's death, and has listened

[1] Oman, *Grace and Personality* (first edition), p. 198.

with relief and humility and gratitude, knows that God pardons iniquity, that His property is always to have mercy. For manifestly God is there linking Himself with our sinful spirits in their sorest trouble, and it requires no argument to prove that He who in boundless love dies for our sins will certainly forgive them. Now it is that Divine compassion, revealed at unspeakable cost, which is received by us in faith. Not that we receive pardon and nothing more ; very far otherwise. We are receiving all our days— peace, courage, the power to love and serve, contagious joy, and a thousand things besides. But they all are, as it were, announced and prophesied in pardon ; for there, as in Jesus' parable, the Father is saying to us : " Son, thou art ever with Me, and all that I have is thine." In a word, forgiveness is the blessing that leads in all other blessings by the hand.

Our problem then is this—Where lies the moral inspiration of that penitent surrender to God which we have found faith to be ? What renewing stimulus is given by that experience ? Or, in still plainer English, why does forgiveness make people good ? It is a tremendously crucial question, for just at this point the whole moral credit of Christianity is at stake. If we are going to have a good conscience about the Gospel, intellectually speaking, whether we hold it for ourselves or offer it to others, we have got to see lucidly that forgiveness does make men good, and why. Let us fasten our thoughts on this for a moment.

We are inquiring exactly how and why faith in a holy yet forgiving God stimulates moral goodness. The first consideration I plead is that all the probabilities are in favour of supposing that it does do this, because *every* genuine faith is stimulating. The test of belief is action. If I believe my house is on fire, I am immediately impelled to try and get my family safely out. If I believe in democracy, I vote for democratic measures; it is the least I can do. And—again assuming that the faith is sincere and heartfelt— if I believe in God, I put myself in line with His purposes. In this general sense, then, we may well take up our problem positively prejudiced in favour of the view that faith in God's redeeming pardon will change my life in definite ways. But we must go further.

Let us start with an elementary thought. The man who has not yet found God is at heart a lonely man; and the more in earnest he is about self-mastery, the more acutely, nay the more bitterly, the loneliness is felt. Moreover, just in proportion to his felt loneliness he is weak, because self-absorbed. Being thus lonely and self-absorbed he is perpetually being tempted, if keen about living right, to brood over failure, occasionally perhaps to brood over success—any-how to be occupied with himself, his moral struggles and relapses. And one decisive result of faith is to turn him right away from all that and *take his mind off himself*. The man of faith has placed his centre of gravity at a new point. In principle, in longing and desire and fundamental choice—I do not say in finished achievement—he is done with self; he has made up his mind for God. In other words, faith by very nature looks outward, away from one's personal defeats and victories—these last being possibly the more dangerous of the two. The soul has been led out of self-absorption, be it despair or pride, and placed in a non-self-centred world.

Further, we saw that what faith accepts from God is pre-eminently His pardon of sin. He has given Himself to us compassionately notwithstanding our treachery. Now at last we have an assurance of His love that goes deeper than our evil; that covers not isolated acts only but the personality, not sins only but the sinner, not the past only but time and eternity. Is not this going to enrich our moral resources? Surely there is such a thing as gratitude, and surely too when men are deeply grateful they show it by what they do. Anyone can see that if once a man knows himself forgiven, by God's sheer goodness, his courage and his hope in struggling with evil are redoubled. The balance of power in the conflict has shifted; now he is in league with God. For the depression of moral effort there is nothing anywhere to compare with the dead grinding weight of conscious guilt; nor is there anything to light the fires of moral energy like the perception that, out of simple Divine love, our guilt has been swept away. Jesus saw this and constantly acted on it. It is because He had said " Thy

sins are forgiven thee " that He added " Go and
sin no more." True, this novel power to obey is
only translated gradually into life and character,
for human life is a scene, always, of development ;
but that obvious and desirable circumstance does
not in the least affect its presence as an effectual
principle from the first.

And once more. There is a fine sentence in
Mrs Sinclair Stevenson's book on Jainism to the
effect that what God has done through the Incarnation is to offer His personal friendship to every man,
woman and child upon the earth. Now we know
quite well what a noble friendship may do for men ;
we also know what the lack of it can mean for
one who is hard pressed by temptation. Of this
or that acquaintance we have heard people say,
" He lost faith in such a one, and went to pieces."
And on the other hand, when we are seeking to
aid another's conflict, how we instinctively look
round for a friend who will not preach to him, but
live steadily at his side. Just such a friend,
steadfast, unweariedly loyal, infinitely strong and
patient, faith possesses from the start in Jesus
Christ. We must never forget that faith is
more by far than imitation, though imitation is
a part of it. Faith means life shared with Christ,
in willing and reverent dependence ; and this
fellowship of life is equivalent to our becoming
partners in Christ's overcoming energies. Thus
anyone who asked doubtfully what moral inspiration there could be in being united to Christ must
have put the question simply because he did not

know or had forgotten who Christ is and what faith means. You cannot believe in Christ, as the New Testament counts believing, without by that act beginning to adopt an attitude to God and righteousness and sin which resembles, at first doubtless most imperfectly, His attitude. Amongst all divergences of opinion within the Church—and Christians have quarrelled over many subjects—there is no subject on which such widespread and enthusiastic unanimity prevails as the triumphant power flowing from Christ's unfailing presence to tempted men. Candid and eager faith makes men free and able to stop sinning —this is a fact as fully certified as the law of gravitation.

IV

Two concluding remarks about Christian faith as we have envisaged it in this chapter may be ventured.

(1) To the believer in his hours of best insight it is self-evidencing. I do not say this is always and uninterruptedly the case. No: the most keen and loyal have their dark days ; their religious life may exhibit " tidal movements of devoutest awe sinking anon to farthest ebb of doubt." Well, even when we personally are traversing such times of eclipse, we can still rejoice that for others the sun is shining on undimmed in the fulness of its strength. M. Maurice Barrès somewhere tells of a young French officer who on leaving for the

front made this last request of his mother : " When the troops come home victorious through the Arc de Triomphe, if I am no longer amongst them, put on your best apparel, and be there."

But in our clear hours of active faith, as our nature lies open, we know with perfect certainty that we are standing face to face with the living God, and that He is receiving us. " The Spirit testifies along with our own spirit that we are children of God." As we gaze on a great picture and its meaning sinks down into our mind, it is not the testimony of artistic tradition merely, or the wondering exclamations of friends beside us, that tell us it is beautiful ; it makes its own adequate impression. So Christ shines by His own light.

(2) Self-evidencing though it be by independent truth, Christian faith finds support in a multitude of analogies drawn from the whole range of man's higher life. We believe, for example, in the ideals of righteousness and purity ; we believe in the power of all such ideals to mould and enrich the world ; we believe in our country, its mission and its responsibility ; we believe in a federated Humanity as, under God, the great hope of a distracted and enfeebled and agonising race. In these and other like cases we are dealing not with any vision of the senses, compelling perception of an object which no sane person can ignore ; nor are we dealing with some theoretic or logical conclusion, which it is impossible to deny or question without a manifest breach of the laws

of thought. We have to do, rather, in all such instances, with great unseen realities, to which the best in us responds, of which we are assured with an assurance that shapes and directs our action, and which demonstrate their power more irresistibly every day that we submit life to their guidance. Thus, it appears, there exist, scattered over the lower slopes that lead up to the great summit, varied lesser analogies and approaches to the redeeming faith by which men grasp God in Christ. God, from the outset of life, puts us as it were in training for the last and complete act of self-committal to Unseen Reality —to that Love of our God and Father which like a canopy overarches all we are and hope for.

Chapter IV : Christianity a Corporate Life.

THE general train of thought in which we have been engaged throughout the preceding chapters may now be summarised briefly. In the first place, we attempted to survey those aspects of human need, felt in every age, which give God's love an opening and make the Gospel something to be welcomed. Next we tried to understand how God came forth to meet this need, revealing Himself, acting in love within history, drawing life after life into His fellowship. Thereafter we embarked on a study of man's response to God's search, inquiring precisely in what ways faith recreates life and enables men to think and act as sons of the Father. In this chapter I should like to supplement all that in a necessary fashion by bringing out the truth that living Christianity, so conceived, is by nature social and corporate and cannot really exist in any other form.

It is because we cannot say everything all at once that we have had to take this point last. But although it comes second in order, it is not secondary. People occasionally talk as if full authentic Christianity could be lived on a desert sland, and as if sharing the religious life of the community, or the Church, was somehow fortuitous. The Christian religion accordingly seems to be essentially individualist, accidentally social. Well, even Robinson Crusoe was incomplete for his

creator's purpose till he had been joined by man
Friday ; and it is quite clear that if you take
any New Testament list of Christian " graces,"
half of them, like love, long-suffering, gentleness
and patience, have no meaning and could never
be put in exercise apart from the common life in
which believers share. What we are now to
discuss is therefore in no sense peripheral or un-
important but belongs to the central realities of
believing experience. The place of the social
character of Christian religion is not in a footnote,
but right in the text ; and this will become
clearer, I hope, at each successive point of the
argument.

I

It would indeed be strange if Christianity had
no corporate or social character, for, as everybody knows, this character invariably belongs to
human life as such. Our independence and our
communal relationship are in no sense rivals ;
each is only actualised and maintained through
the instrumentality of the other. Just as two
athletes can only wrestle by clinging together, in
action and reaction, and nobody can wrestle all
by himself, so it is here : society exists through
individual personalities and their bearing on one
another, while conversely it is only within society,
and as supported by its larger life, that strong
individuality can flourish. Break society in frag-
ments, and personality in the true sense vanishes.

The claim is occasionally made by thoughtless
people that what you really want for a just
world is that everybody should get exactly what
he deserves—no less, no more. Mercifully, however, we are none of us dealt with on that
principle. What in the name of reason have we
done, for example, to *deserve* the present position
and triumphs of medical science ? We only get
the benefit of it through our doctor when we ask
him to call, but there can be no talk of "deserving"
anything. Or in what sense do we deserve that
the marshes which used to cover much of the
surface of the country should have been drained
and malaria stamped out, or that a national
system of roads should have been established,
or modern education ? There has been no merit
of ours in all these cases. What happens is simply
that we benefit incessantly by the solidarity of the
race, by the continuity of the generations storing
up past gains ; and we accept as of course all
the good things which come through the medium
of inheritance. At times we complain, bitterly
and with bewilderment, when we are called upon
to suffer because our life is bound up inextricably
with the life of others ; but in sober truth our
progress, our happiness, our very possession of a
moral character, are all of them directly dependent
on the very laws of solidarity against which we cry
out in revolt only at moments when their sharp
edge touches us to the quick. "No man liveth
to himself." It has been truly said that unless
we are prepared to accept a system in which we

are all unrelated atoms, and no social system
possible—indeed no world at all such as we know—
the innocent must suffer for and with the guilty,
must take the bitter with the sweet ; and when
the balance is struck, the advantages entirely out-
weigh the disadvantages, and those advantages
are mainly unearned and undeserved by the
recipients. It is on these lines of social action
and reaction, then, that everything we call human
life is planned ; and the idea cannot even be enter-
tained that Christianity should form an exception
and be based on the principle of isolation.

If, again, we take one vital factor of experience
apart from which true religion is unthinkable,
viz., the attainment of moral character, we shall
find this also to be indissociably bound up with a
life which others share. For the moment let us
put aside all we know of ethics and consider
simply how we behave by instinct towards those
whose moral nature is still undeveloped—young
children, wild or undisciplined persons, and those
in non-Christian lands whom we seek to win for
Christ. At once we recognise that what they most
need is to be surrounded with people of character.
We say of this or that hooligan—What he wants
is a good friend. There can be no doubt at all
that only in fellowship with others can a change
come for the better. It is not enough to say,
there are germs of goodness in him which will
spring up and flourish by spontaneous vitality, or
he has natural principles of conscience which will
automatically assert their power. Life does not

work out that way. Of course it is the fact that every individual has a rudimentary moral nature derived from God, the Source of all goodness, and that apart from this basis of ethical potentiality, to which appeal can be made, moral influence and training would go for nothing. But the point is that all this natural basis *does* go for nothing except in so far as it is evoked, sustained, developed by personal fellowship. Without fellowship it is like an uprooted plant. Torn from its moorings, the plant does not die instantly ; for a time it may survive : but even a child knows that unless it is speedily replaced in the soil its fate is sealed ; it has no prospect whatever of living on. Similarly, we shall search in vain for a human being now possessed of genuinely moral character who has not been helped forward to that by better men than himself, in the shadow of whose stronger personality his immature nature at first grew up.

Memory corroborates this for each of us. The beginnings of conscious aspiration, of self-knowledge, self-reproach and self-control, have been for every one of us deeply involved in the acquaintance of good men and women. It is what we saw in them that wakened us. Had we lived in isolation, and been left to sink or swim as we could, moral insight and the first steps of moral effort would have possessed no meaning or reality our minds could apprehend. The common gathering-ground for the living waters both of morality and religion is in *personal fellowship*. All higher life rests on corporate antecedents. "To reverence persons, to bow inwardly at the presence of moral power and goodness, is the root of all true religion." No man holds by the infinite worth of truth except by contagion from those to whom truth is sacred. No man loves purity who does not mingle with the pure. That is why the impulse of hero-worship in a boy is of such incalculable importance. Wherever it is present, it means that within the circle of human influence playing upon his life that young heart has discovered some one to whose character he pays the homage of his being, confessing that here at least he has encountered that which is absolutely real and absolutely precious, and which therefore has become for him a trustworthy guide to life's true meaning. Such reverence for persons forms the seed of, as well as the preparation for, a satisfying faith in God.

Let us pursue this idea for a moment. Somebody once stated the difference between Romanism and Evangelical Protestantism by saying that according to Romanism you come to Christ by first coming to the Church, whereas for Protestantism you come to the Church by coming in the first place to Christ. This mode of putting things is unsatisfactory or incomplete, and for this reason. In Protestant circles—though not in the teaching of the great Reformers—religious individualism, it can hardly be denied, has often been rampant. Too frequently the soul was pictured as isolated, or virtually isolated, in its approach to and its dealings with the love of God in Christ. Men were so keen to bring out the spiritual independence of each life that they tended to overlook, not to say deny, the social quality and nature of personal Christianity from first to last. And the question may well suggest itself whether one reason for hesitation about making the Christian decision felt by persons in non-Christian countries who realised keenly the attraction of the Gospel might not be owing to the fact that they shrank from the spiritual loneliness or isolation to which, quite mistakenly, they imagined they were being invited. In their old religion at least they formed part of a community, which held them up and sustained their religious belief and practice on every side ; was it not a loss, they may have asked, and a loss for which only very doubtful gains were being offered in compensation, that now they should be expected to stand before God all by themselves, unsupported and uncheered by the common life of the whole body ? If they felt this, we can see their feeling to have been wholly erroneous. It points to a conception of Christianity which has no resemblance to the New Testament, and which besides is utterly unlike the living faith to which we all of us owe our best possessions.

As to the New Testament there can be no doubt of any kind. Everything that Jesus said concerning the Kingdom of God, everything taught by St Paul or other primitive writers about the Church as the Body of Christ, comes in here.

The New Testament shows no interest whatever in unattached Christians. It takes for granted that Christ's followers will hold together, that they share each other's life, and that apart from the mutual giving and receiving of the brethren they would not be what they are, but something quite different. Everything starts with the fact that the apostles' preaching of the Risen Lord gathered men and women in a fellowship of faith and love around His Person. They were one at all because one in Him. To use again the infinitely suggestive figure, the Church is His Body ; that is to say, it is a living whole, all parts of the whole draw life and power from the same Divine source, and, in this living character, it forms the active instrument or organ of Christ in getting His will accomplished for the world. Just as you cannot say "citizen" without implying the State, so, the New Testament teaches, you cannot say "Christian" without in turn implying the Church. Thus the Church, in the classical picture of Christian religion, is a Divine society called into existence by Christ for purposes of His own, and by its instrumentality His influence as Redeemer is propagated from one generation to another.

Does not experience confirm this view ? If we make a careful effort to remember our own religious history, and to scrutinise the factors that entered and made it what it is, what do we find ? We invariably find, I think, that Christian life began for us through the influence of persons—whether parents or friends—who evoked our reverence, our trust, our desire to imitate. Through them we became aware of a possible life higher than the senses and nobler than worldliness ; through them, too, we were led into the Christian fellowship and realised that this fellowship, by its helps and supports, had been doing a very great deal for us long before we could appreciate its value. And thus our faith sprang out of the Church's life ; the Church here being understood not as a legally organised corporation, but as " the company of believing people," the society of those who, as the New Testament puts it, call on the name of Jesus Christ. All that we have and are as Jesus' disciples has come to us through this channel ; and to recognise the fact is mere fairness. If this be so, we can better understand the old writer who declares, " he who has not the Church for his Mother cannot have God for his Father." Or take the words of Calvin, a free spirit if ever there was one : " Let us learn by the mere name of mother how profitable, indeed how necessary, is the knowledge of her ; since there is no other entrance into life unless she herself conceive us in her womb, unless she bear us, unless she foster us at her breast, unless she guard us under her care and government, until we put off this mortal flesh, and become like the angels." That looks a trifle strong, but is it not after all pretty near the truth ? No one supposes, for example, that personal Christianity leaps up suddenly by what biologists call spon-taneous generation in the mind of a Zulu or a Maori, quite independently of the efforts of

Christians to bring Christ to their attention. Wherever people have come to Christian faith, be it in South Africa or in England, it is because other Christians went out and won them to the common reception of the love of God in Christ Jesus, which is the bond uniting all members of the Church to each other. Religion is so essentially corporate and social that it permeates the world only through the spreading infection of a shared life. God works, in short, through truth and personality. He has left it dependent on us whether it shall be possible for Him to do His greatest works. That is the glory of discipleship, and that is also its responsibility.

A striking contrast to all this is Mysticism. There is no need to entangle ourselves in the question whether out-and-out Mysticism can be Christian ; but we may start from the point that since well-developed Mysticism is to be found in Greece, India, Islam and China, it cannot be something *distinctive* of Christianity. Now, missionary experience has invariably gone to show that in propaganda only what is distinctively Christian really counts. People cannot be at the Christian level who have never heard Jesus' name. In its characteristic forms, as in Neo-platonism or great mediæval writers like Scotus Erigena, Mysticism exhibits two marked features. In the first place, it is more than half indifferent to the historical revelation of God, and is therefore bound to give to Jesus Christ a merely secondary place. It is in fact a sort of philosophical religion, which turns from history to find God solely within. Secondly (and it is of significance that the two things should go together), it does not conceive religion socially, or feed its experience, as our Lord did, on the devout life of previous ages. The mystic tends to be what Wordsworth called himself, a "Solitary." At the height of devotion, he stands alone ; he has cast off the human ties ; he faces God in pure abstract independence, not as a member of the Christian family. Speaking broadly, then, the Mysticism of ancient religion, as of Indian piety still, has these two negative features : absence of the great thought that God manifests His mind through history, and a corresponding failure to perceive that He has a kingdom to be realised in the world through the service of believing men and their corporate activity. The juxta-position of these two defects is precisely what we might expect. No man can indulge apathy towards the working of God in ages behind us without succumbing also to apathy regarding His purpose for the world around us. If our religion neglects history, it will neglect society as well.

II

From what has now been said, two consequences follow. First of all, Christianity loses its moral nerve if it be made independent of the historical stream of believing life. It is unreal and unintelligible apart from the revelation of God in bygone events and persons, above all in Christ, and

its redeeming powers are invariably brought close
to us through the contagious touch of those who
are carrying on the vital tradition. Further—
another aspect of the same truth—our religion is
indissolubly linked up, in action and reaction, with
the society of which Christ is centre and head.
Each new personality grows out of the family of
God, and in turn makes his contribution to its
growth. The Church does not pass with the
passing forward of its individual members. This
principle may be illustrated from more than one
side.

(1) First, as regards Christian truth in its
entirety. There are to-day in the world differing
versions of Christianity ; fuller Christianity, as we
may call it, and Christianity that may be described
as reduced or diluted. Some people hold that
Jesus Christ is but the first Christian, the great
Pioneer of trust in the Father, whose trust we are
called to imitate—*this and nothing more ;* which
is what I mean by Christianity in a diluted form.
Others, while asserting with emphasis all that the
former class believe, hold that Christ is a Divine
Saviour, in whom God is personally present to
deliver man by the sacrificial conquest of sin and
death—One whose faith we cannot even *try* to
share without discovering that for a triumphant
religious life we have got to believe *in* Him as well
as *like* Him, and that through this attachment to
Himself He empowers us to be God's obedient
sons—which is what I mean by Christianity of
the fuller sort. Now a good deal could be said

for the position that while the first kind of Gospel might suffice for this or that individual, nothing but the second kind will supply a real basis for the Church. You cannot erect a Church which will attain any appreciable success in building the Kingdom of God on earth through the long generations anywhere save on the basis of faith in the crucified and risen Lord. Christian history makes that fairly clear. Why, then, is it that *individuals* can carry on not unsuccessfully, at least for a time, with a more attenuated Gospel? Just because, by partaking in the life of the organic society, and mingling with its worship, they get the benefit of the richer and fuller convictions by which it is sustained. Their experience is all the time being fed from larger and deeper springs outside themselves ; impulses and energies accrue to them from the corporate whole ; they find daily in their associates more striking instances of brave belief and therefore better reasons for believing ; the atmosphere of a more abundant life is around them as something they can breathe and assimilate. Whereas the isolated man has to do everything for himself and receives less as he gradually comes to impart nothing at all. Not a few Christians at the moment are being tempted to take up with somewhat genial and shallow ideas of God ; they think, or tend to think, of the Divine Fatherhood wholly apart from the Cross and hence without that encompassing light of awe-inspiring moral passion in which the Father appears in the New Testament. And if it were not for profounder thoughts drawn from the long experience of Christ's Church, which is far older than any of us, the danger might be a very real one of a poor, superficialised Gospel being held out to the world as all we have to offer. The community has a bigger truth than any isolated person. Here is a first instance of the fact that Jesus Christ committed His cause not to the separate individual but to a society. The Church holds its new knowledge of God in trust for posterity.

(2) A second example, to go more into detail, is the Forgiveness of Sins. Now it is through the Church, and only so, that we any of us become aware of the great fact that God forgives the sinful. Indeed we should not go far wrong in defining the Church as the society of people who, in view of Jesus, are quite sure that " there is joy in the presence of the angels of God over one sinner who repents." If at this moment we personally believe that sin can be forgiven ; if in our hearts we know that our sin *has* been forgiven and that life to the end can be spent under the overarching canopy of that pardoning love of God ; and if we ask ourselves how we became aware of this, the answer is plain. It was through contact with the followers of Christ. Good men and women conveyed to us by word or bearing the uplifting certainty that we need not grapple with our weakness single-handed, but that God's merciful friendship could be our joy as it was theirs. The flame of their faith set ours on fire. By contagion of their trust in the forgiveness of God we too learned

trust. No man has ever reached this amazing conviction of the Father's pardon in Christ or perceived it to be the most blessed and emancipating thing in the world, except by living beside those who themselves were forgiven, and who let him see it.

All this is sufficiently familiar, but there is a side of the matter which is less so. One influence perpetually leading people to faith in God's pardon is traceable to the fact that, within the Christian society, they find themselves being pardoned for their own faults. Here we cannot lay too great stress upon the capital circumstance that, in the main, the Church is made up of families. For the forgiveness of God is only credible in a certain atmosphere. It must be an atmosphere in which kind and loving mutual forgiveness is *practised*. It is only as people meet with those who do forgive injuries that they dare to rise to the vast and superficially all but unbelievable truth that God forgives. This is one great reason why the Christian Church is in the world at all, and why Christian life, in its roots and its character, is not accidentally but intrinsically corporate. The Church is in the world in order that within its circle of mutual placability people may breathe an air which gives them courage to believe in the pardoning grace of the Father.

The Church as a whole, it was said a moment ago, was composed of families. What significance does this have for our purpose now ? Surely this —that those who in the believing fellowship are presented with the life-giving message of Forgiveness, in the majority of cases listen with hearts prepared and tuned to the Gospel by their experience of pardon in the circle of loving and patient friendship which we call *home*. They have known what it means for a mother or father to forgive their childish faults. They have learnt that the world is such that pardon can and does happen; that the nature of human life is not of a kind to veto forgiveness among friends; that broken relations between persons can be reconstituted. In their life at home they have tasted and seen the reality of love's supreme act—the sweeping away, by the free pardon of offences, of obstacles to the unity of hearts. If those who love me have once pardoned my young disobedience and follies, then ever after I have in my heart that which interprets for me the loving-kindness of God in taking my sins away. I am not any longer living in a world ruled throughout by such physical necessities that there is no room for any moral experience. Provided I do not shut my mind utterly against the thought of God, it is now impossible for me to imagine that pardon is no more than a sentimental expression. I *have* been forgiven; I have gained the all-deciding insight that good men and women do forgive; and in spirit I have knelt before them, acknowledging that such love is the greatest thing in the world. Through the goodness of my friends, bearing with my evil and refusing in spite of it to cast me off, and knowing thus how to deal with wrong so as

G

to rob it of its estranging power and renew in love the bonds which it had broken, my mind has opened, or has prepared to open, to the forgiving love of God the Father. And in this great experience, or series of experiences, there lies another vital proof that only through the fellowship of the corporate life of Christian disciples can the full wonder of redemption be apprehended or enjoyed.

(3) A third reality on which, if we view it from this angle, a fresh light seems to fall, is the central fact of the Holy Spirit. Some three or four years back a little book was written by Mr Roland Allen under the title *Pentecost and the World*. He there argued that the Holy Spirit, especially in the Acts of the Apostles, is exhibited as in essence a missionary Spirit. That men should be impelled by the Spirit to agonise for the redemption of their fellows is no accident ; it is as characteristic of the Spirit's work as teaching or sanctification. When we open the New Testament we perceive that people living the Spirit-filled life felt an irrepressible desire to impart that which they had received ; the Spirit revealed to them the world's absolute need of the Gospel and enabled them to supply the need ; and under this direct higher guidance they went out farther and ever farther into the Gentile world, overcoming prejudices of their own which might have hindered their witness or prevented them from receiving into communion men often the most remote from themselves in habits of life or thought. So that when we ask

the question frequently put in sheer bewilderment, What *is* the Holy Spirit ? a summary but so far perfectly sound reply is to say : The Holy Spirit is just the Spirit operating in every effort to save men. Which after all is very natural. The Holy Spirit, let us remember, is not simply a compendious name for conscience or for the generalities of religious experience. The Spirit, truly understood, is the Spirit of redeeming Love that animated Jesus Christ. *He* gives to men the selfsame Spirit that lived in Himself.

This is a fresh exhilarating note. We are apt to conceive the Spirit as a purely personal possession, issuing in an individual perfection of character which has no vital bond with the wider outlook of humanity and the world-wide Kingdom of God. When however we turn to the New Testament what do we find ? We find that the Spirit is always figured there as the possession of the believing society. Not of course of the society irrespective of the persons who compose it, but just as definitely not of persons, by themselves and in isolation, irrespective of the rest of society. " All these gifts worketh the one and the same Spirit, dividing to each one severally even as He will." Only in the fellowship of disciples can the powers of Christ's Spirit be fully displayed. St Paul's account of what, in Dr Moffatt's rendering, is the Spirit's *harvest*—viz. " love, joy, peace, good temper, kindliness, generosity, fidelity, gentleness, self-control "—is obviously (as we saw above) a list of attitudes or affections which in virtually every case demand society for their action. All are generated in the individual Christian mind, but all as plainly move outward and find their object in others. Or, to put it otherwise, what the Spirit is revealed in the New Testament as perpetually doing is to make " saints "; but you will never find the word " saint " occur in the singular. Invariably it is plural. As Denney has said : " The ideal of God's people cannot be adequately realised in, and ought not to be presumptuously claimed by, any single person." Holiness in the proper sense can grow only in the family gathered round Jesus Christ, *i.e.* the Church. The Spirit, in short, is the Spirit of One who did not merely touch and change individual lives, but rather established a Kingdom. His eye was bent upon a community ruled in all its parts by love and righteousness. Hence it is this same Divine Spirit—it can be nothing lower or more commonplace—that sends men ranging out into human life with the one desire to co-operate obediently with Christ in widening the bounds of the brotherhood, by combating ignorance, pride and covetousness, vice and disease, and every social injustice and public wrong.

(4) Lastly, there is the hope of Immortality as Christianity proclaims it.

If we turn over the periodical literature of religion fifty or even thirty years ago, in this country, we shall I expect find that the tone of religious people's thoughts about the eternal prospect—about everything, that is, which we gather up under the word " heaven "—was at that time chiefly, and hence unduly, individualistic. The great question was often felt to be : " Shall I go to heaven ? " or " Has my friend gone there ? " It would be unpardonable to suggest that anything else than what is sacred and loving was implied in this. But none the less the distribution of accent, the perspective, so to call it, is not that of the New Testament, but very far different. It is only in an accidental manner that the New Testament touches upon the purely individual question, the destiny of this or that man. What the Apostles care most for is the triumph of the Kingdom. This is one reason why they so constantly thought and spoke about the Return of Christ. Christ was to come back, not to meet privately with individuals, but to finish and consummate the Kingdom He had founded. His advent was, so to speak, a public or world-embracing event. Thus when these great believers of the first century lifted up their eyes, gazing forward to a new world awaiting them, and anticipating its perfectness, what their hopes mainly clustered round was the completely realised Kingdom of God. The private lot of the single life is not in the least forgotten —how could it be, if God is Father ? But it is caught up and absorbed in the greater and richer expectation of a redeemed order ; an order in which the people of God, freed eternally from sin and weakness and grief, shall serve Him in the unbroken communion of saints.

There is a minor point at which we undoubtedly

gain by recapturing the New Testament attitude
and accent. It is this. People have often asked
the question : Shall we know each other in the
next life ?   Now if individualism be our point of
departure, and if what we are chiefly interested in
the future is the fortunes of this or that believer
(usually ourselves), it is not quite easy to know
what reply to make.   But if, as with the Apostles,
our controlling thought be God and His Kingdom,
and if (as we must) we regard the Kingdom as
closely analogous not to a State but to a family,
the whole difficulty vanishes.   If God is in truth
our Father, we can simply and without concern
rest in the assurance that a Father has of course
around Him the household of His children, and
that it belongs to the very meaning of a family
that its members love each other, and therefore
know each other.

It would do us all good to think of Heaven
more than we ordinarily do.   And that not because
of prospective delights that allure the pleasure-
loving, but for nobler reasons.   Otherworldliness
is no sin ;   on the contrary it is the source of
some of the best and most courageous impulses
that can fill the heart of a man.   As Wordsworth
puts it :

> We live by hope
> And by desire ; we see by the glad light
> And breathe by the sweet air of futurity.

And, to single out one aspect of a theme of infinite
and elusive magnitude, is it not ennobling to dwell
imaginatively on the new and wide richness of

fellowship, on the immortal side of death, that awaits all who are one in Christ ? Nothing in years of war became more afflicting than the sense of alienation from " enemy friends," if the phrase be permissible. We were vividly aware of kinship with them ; we recalled those ties of religion and humanity which could never be destroyed ; yet by their fault or ours we were separated from them and they from us. And apart from such temporary estrangements, how narrow the bounds of human love ! How the essential limits of space and time seem to interpose a veto, and to prevent deep intimacy with multitudes of the good, the wise, the Christlike ! I say it is good to know that these limits, these infirmities of love and care, will not last for ever. Part of Christian faith is this very looking forward to unimpeded union with God, and through Him with all the faithful, and this under conditions that minister to perfect and unending life. Hence " in seasons of calm weather," when the air grows clear, we may have sight of distant horizons and the great mountains of God. In such hours we shall reckon in wonder and in hope on the new friendships appointed for us there, and dream perhaps that the Father may choose to send out His perfected family of earth on missions of love and succour to other worlds.

Date Due

11/24/			